Is He Lying to You?

Is He Lying to You?

An Ex-CIA Polygraph Examiner Reveals What Men Don't Want You to Know

INCLUDES MORE THAN 101 EXAMPLES OF DECEPTION

Dan Crum
"THE DATING DETECTIVE"

CAREER PRESS

Franklin Lakes, N.J.

Copyright © 2010 by Dan Crum

IS HE LYING TO YOU?
EDITED AND TYPESET BY KARA KUMPEL
Cover design by Howard Grossman / 12E Design
Printed in the U.S.A. by Courier

To order this title, please call toll-free 1-800-CAREER-1 (NJ and Canada: 201-848-0310) to order using VISA or MasterCard, or for further information on books from Career Press.

The Career Press, Inc., 3 Tice Road, PO Box 687,
Franklin Lakes, NJ 07417
www.careerpress.com

Library of Congress Cataloging-in-Publication Data
Crum, Dan.
   Is he lying to you? : an ex-CIA polygraph examiner reveals what men don't want you to know / by Dan Crum.
      p. cm.
   Includes index.
   ISBN 978-1-60163-103-9
   ISBN 978-1-60163-751-2
   1. Dating (Social customs)--Psychological aspects. 2. Man woman relationships--Psychological aspects. 3. Deception. 4. Truthfulness and falsehood. I. Title.

HQ801.C755 2010
646.7'7--dc22

                                                        2009050333

Don't Just Date—Investigate!

Acknowledgments

I t is because of the significant contributions made by other people that this book exists. I want to thank God for blessing me with a mind that refuses to accept things as they are and a desire to find a way to make things better.

I want to thank my family: my wife, Cindy, who is an incredible mother to our four children—Grace, Madeline, Will, and Abby—and a very supportive wife; my father, Rick Crum (FBI Special Agent–retired), who taught me the value of hard work and a positive attitude and always led by example; my mother, Joan Crum, who taught me to have compassion for others and made sure to remind me that "it is good to be right, but it is right to be good," and is a living saint whom you would be fortunate to meet; my brothers—Richard, Matt, Brian, and Kevin—who helped me establish a competitive spirit, and with whom I learned the value of working as a team; and my younger sister, Anne Kelley, who helped inspire the idea for this book through my desire to help her navigate through life with the ability to identify deception and make informed decisions.

In addition I would like to thank Bill Fairweather (Chief of Polygraph Division, CIA–retired) for introducing me to the art of detecting deception and helping me start my career in the CIA. I want to thank Barry McManus (Chief Polygraph Examiner, CIA–retired) for trusting me to represent him and his courses.

Finally, I want to thank my agent, Bob Diforio, Career Press and their amazing team, and Rusty Fischer, who was a major contributor to this book.

Contents

About This Book

I s he lying to you?

According to recent statistics, the chances are very good that he is. According to Tim Cole of DePaul University, "Most individuals (92 percent) admit having lied to a romantic partner or can recall an occasion where they were not completely honest...."

Of course, not all lying is created equal. Asking your date how much he earns per year might result in the confident reply of "Six figures!" Well, earning $100,000 a year is *technically* six figures (and far from shabby), but it's a long way from making $250,000 annually (which is more along the lines of the "six figures" he was probably implying). So, did he just lie? And, more importantly, how many half-truths, omissions, or evasions are you willing to overlook in a romantic partner?

If you're like most people, the answer is plenty. Adds Cole, "When not explicitly deceiving partners, many people acknowledge withholding information or trying to avoid certain issues altogether."

I want to change all that.

From the CIA to the Singles Scene:
The Dating Detective

I used to conduct polygraph exams for the CIA. As an Intelligence Analyst at the National Counterterrorism Center, Terrorist Identities Group, my work was used in support of intelligence assessments for the Executive Office, to include the President in the war on terror. Now I consult people on deception in their everyday lives, be it on the job, at home, or particularly in their relationships.

I have spent my life studying human interactions and identifying deceptive behaviors, and today I'm known as the Dating Detective. I can teach you to determine when someone is lying to you.

Is He Lying to You?

Ask the frustrated single woman what she looks for most in a member of the opposite sex, and she's likely to give an exasperated, one-word answer: honesty. Modern women have been lied to, betrayed, fibbed to, deceived, and disappointed more times than they care to admit, but that's because they've been playing too much defense, and not enough offense.

Don't trust someone just because they look sincere when they say something; don't be fooled by another wolf in designer clothing. Instead, learn the secrets of how the CIA interviews and investigates people to actually know if your date is telling the truth.

Decode the Opposite Sex by What They Do— and Don't—Say

Now it's time to take off the gloves, roll up your sleeves, and take back control of your dating life. I begin by setting up a fictional—but all-too-real—scenario in which one woman (we'll call her "Ashley") is participating in a speed-dating event at her local nightclub.

In this scenario you will act as the Dating Detective to determine your innate ability to identify deceptive behaviors. You will judge the verbal and nonverbal responses of four very different guys. How every guy responds is indicative, at least to me, of whether or not he is telling the truth. I'll leave the results a mystery (for now), and will reveal which of the four men were lying at the end of the book—as well as how to spot the clues right away. In this way, Ashley and every other woman will be able to spot deception just as I can by the final chapter.

Next I'll continue with the very definition of a lie; you'd be surprised by how many ways there are to lie, the degrees of lying, and what, exactly, constitutes a lie. For instance, there is "deletion" and "fallacy," there are various levels of lying, such as "significant" and "harmless," and, finally, there are four specific reasons guys will lie, such as "preservation," "privacy," or even "courtesy."

Then I will introduce my Get REELL Strategy, which will guide you to use your senses in a whole new way. This strategy comes in handy with my next big revelation: everybody lies! I'll teach you not to look for truthful behavior, but instead to be on the lookout for deception.

I'll continue by introducing the concept of your "Window of Focus," which can help you spot the difference between "What Is Normal" behavior and what— and when—to look and listen for. From there I introduce the Two Biggest Signs of Deception: sleep points and guilt twists. With these two signs alone, I contend, *anyone* can spot deception, even on their very first try.

Next comes one of the book's biggest features: a real-life, real-time list of more than 101 examples of verbal deception. Now you can know what to be on the lookout for, and, just as importantly, what to listen for when one of these pops up. From verbal we shift to the nonverbal, with a chapter on nonverbal deception titled "Liar's Moves."

And finally, the conclusion of the speed date. Here I'll expose which men were telling the truth and who was being deceptive. Lastly, I provide three advanced concepts to help you put the lessons you've just learned into real-life scenarios with such sections as "Setting the Stage," "Rapport," and "Trusting Your Intuition."

Don't Just Date—Investigate!

When you use my strategies for detecting deception, you will immediately gain more control over your future; these strategies can be applied to all of your interactions with men, including dating, committed relationships, and even marriage.

What's more, they work as well in the boardroom as they do in the bedroom; women who learn these strategies can be better employees, coworkers, negotiators, bosses, and businesspeople. By looking for deception rather than honesty, you, too, can detect deception at any time, in any place.

Can You Handle the Truth?

The suspect licks his lips and stares at his shoes. His hands rest on the table in front of him, or, occasionally, fly to his knees. The light is purposefully dim, the air temperature carefully controlled. The interrogator tunes out the background noise to focus on the suspect's responses.

During the interrogation, the suspect intermittently tugs at his tie, fiddles with his watch, and crosses his legs. Upon termination of the interrogation he tries to make light of the scenario; too often, his deception is so complete as to fool even the most experienced interrogator.

Another interrogation is scheduled, with similar results.

No, this is not some nightmare scenario out of my first day on the job as a former CIA Polygraph Examiner and Investigator. Unfortunately, this is just one more man deceiving one more woman on the modern dating scene—or, in an equal number of cases, at the family dinner table or even in the bedroom.

The setting is not some sterile interrogation room but the local watering hole. The interrogator is neither an expert nor actively looking for deception. The suspect knows this all too well.

Ladies, if this scenario sounds eerily familiar, then you've come to the right place.

Is He Lying to You?

If you're picking up, buying, and now reading a book titled *Is He Lying to You?* no doubt you already know—or at least suspect—the answer. In this, you are not alone. In a recent poll conducted by a top dating Website, 78 percent of respondents answered no to the question, "On a date, do you think your companion is generally 100-percent truthful?" When asked, "Do you trust someone when you first date them?" 67 percent of respondents again answered in the negative.

Although these sobering statistics are somewhat depressing, my experience tells me they're all too accurate. When I was a polygraph examiner and investigator for the CIA, my duties involved detecting deception on a daily basis; even after my initial, intensive training, I continued to attend countless classes, briefings, conferences, and seminars at some of the country's most elite schools, and became an expert in the art of detecting deception.

As I interviewed, polygraphed, and interrogated countless subjects during the course of my career, I often realized that these skills were sorely missing from and definitely needed out in the real world. I began to notice a not-so-joyful refrain among my many single and even not-so-single female friends: "Is he lying to me?"

Some friends knew of my CIA experience; others didn't. I believe they were asking me simply as a man, to see my take on the situation. I responded with much clearer insight than my friends had, and, even based on hearsay evidence or from a distance, I could, more often than not, respond in the affirmative to that question based on the evidence at hand.

"Yes," I would answer soberly, "he *is* lying to you."

Learn the Basic Strategies for Detecting Deception

It occurred to me that there could be a second use for my CIA experience other than just idle conversation at cocktail parties. I sat down and tried to put myself in the shoes of a modern woman active in her local singles scene or the doubtful woman confronting her husband about her suspicions.

What would she need to know? I asked myself. *How could she detect deception without all the tools I had at my disposal in the CIA?* I knew that to devise a system that would allow everyday civilian women to become, in effect, Dating Detectives, I would have to make it simple, straightforward, and available to everyone.

After much trial and error, I developed the system found in this book, which will take you on a journey as you navigate through life experiencing deception in its many forms. Along the way you will learn how deception looks and sounds. In the end, you will be prepared to face all the deception that surrounds you.

Don't Just Date—Investigate!

There's a great line in the movie *A Few Good Men* from Jack Nicholson: "You can't *handle* the truth!"

Ladies, can *you* handle the truth?

If you're reading this book, I can only assume that you (a) have been lied to in the past, (b) fear you're being lied to now, and/or (c) are concerned about being lied to in the future.

If any of these describe your situation, then I have four words for you: don't just date—investigate!

Far too often, women go on dates expecting the handsome prince to ride up on the white horse and whisk her off to a fairy land where they'll both live happily ever after. And even after the new romance has faded and you find yourself sitting across from your husband of 20 years, you still want to see him as your knight in shining armor.

Ladies, here's a hint: guys know this!

Frankly, they count on it.

Most men—scratch that, most *deceptive* men—know you'll be so busy noticing their polished shoes, fat wallet, nicely trimmed goatee, and fancy class ring that you'll ignore the lack of interest in their eyes, the rote patter of their answers, or even the outright deception in their voices.

Now, don't get me wrong—there are plenty of good guys out there, and in learning to spot deception in the bad ones, you'll notice honesty, consideration, sincerity, and compassion in the good ones; obviously, being able to spot Mr. Right is a valuable tool.

So is spotting deception before you fall for Mr. Wrong.

So maybe my language is a little harsh, maybe my examples are a tad depressing, and maybe the lesson I've got to teach is a little sobering: *Learn it anyway*. You bought this book because you already suspect you're being lied to.

Won't it be a waste of time—and money—if you're not ready to handle the truth?

Combat Deception With an Action Plan for Life

Don't worry; I've taken the hassle out of finding the truth. Not only will I assist you in this crash course on deception, but I will walk you step-by-step through this system, and you will make all the choices and, ultimately, take all the action.

Before we get started, let's address one more issue. Again, this is about you, because this whole book is about you: Are you truly committed to reading this book in its entirety and using this system in your life?

If your answer is no, don't waste your time reading any further. I won't be disappointed. In fact, I expect that some of you have never read a complete book since you were in school. You probably just bought this book because you heard Oprah talking about men who lie or because it is a best-seller. You're part of that group of people, huh?

Stop! I am hoping your answer is a passionate "Yes, I'm truly committed!" I pray that you are in that elite group of individuals who read books such as this to make their lives better. If you're not, decide now to commit to this book, for better or for worse. Your path to relationship success starts with this one simple step.

You're committed? Great! Give yourself a high-five. I'm serious; no one's looking. Do it.

Now let's get down to business: *This book is going to change your life*. It is going to change your life in an area that we all care about most: relationships. Are you ready? Great, now follow my directions carefully.

Action Plan for the Introduction

Get a journal or notebook. As I give you assignments, do them in this journal. For your first assignment, write on the first page of this journal:

I, [your name], am deciding right now to commit to love myself enough to read this book in its entirety and do all the action steps the author describes. I will then apply what I learn to my life and, in turn, I will be prepared to identify deception.

FREE BONUS: Go to *www.lyingbook.com/bonuses* and download a digital journal that includes the action steps for each chapter.

That's it, you made it. You have reached the end of the Introduction; now it's time to start reading the book. Get excited! I know you're going to absolutely love this book. In fact, I guarantee you that after you read it, do the action steps, apply them to your life, and start identifying deception, you'll tell everyone about it.

Go for it—just try and prove me wrong!

CHAPTER 1

Can You Spot the Liar?

The cruelest lies are often told in silence.
—Robert Louis Stevenson

Speed dating is a fairly recent phenomenon, beginning in California in the late 1990s, but it caught on fast and has since become a permanent fixture of the modern dating landscape. Today you can find speed-dating events all over the world, and, if you don't stumble upon one yourself in your efforts to start or possibly relaunch your love life, a quick Google of the keywords "speed dating" can set you up with a local directory where you are likely to find dozens of events in your neck of the woods.

And with good reason: for many, speed dating is an opportunity to fit a lot of blind dates—sometimes up to a dozen—in one sitting. For the busy, shy, or awkward woman, here in one setting—typically a local restaurant, nightclub, or bar, but increasingly in a community rec center or church social hall—you can quickly, conveniently, and safely interact with a variety of men in one setting, on one night.

For me, though, speed dating has always been a veritable Petri dish of deceptive behavior. What's worse, the more men speed date, the easier it is for them to become deceptive. On any given night a male speed dater can interact with a dozen or more women.

If his desire is to be deceptive—and, again, I'm not saying every single guy in the world is out there looking to get one over on you—but if a guy *wants* to be deceptive, there is no better "beginner's course" on the planet than your typical speed-dating event.

Here he can quickly perfect his patter, learn what works and what doesn't, and, with each unsuspecting woman, gradually evolve to become the ultimate deception machine by night's end.

For instance, what worked on Woman #1 may, with just a slight enhancement of delivery, work even better on Woman #2. What didn't go so well on Woman #3 can be dropped by the time he's in front of Woman #4 or #5, making his patter practically error-free by Woman #8 or #9 of the night. And by the last few women of the evening? Well, ladies, look out: you're likely to be deceived.

Dating Detective: *The Home Version*

Enter one of my best Dating Detective students, "Ashley." Ashley is in her 30s, never married, looking for Mr. Right, and tired of the "meat market" scene she had to endure in her early- to mid-20s. She's eager to find men outside of her comfort zone—her workplace and apartment building.

When Ashley first suggested speed dating, I thought it would be a great idea not only to help her detect deception, but also to help my readers detect it as well. What better way, I reasoned, to expose these deceptive daters than to follow Ashley on a typical night out and show her—and you—which guys were telling the truth and which were being deceptive?

So I made Ashley a deal. I promised her that if she would ask each guy the same two questions at some point during their speed date, and then pay close attention to both their verbal and nonverbal responses, I would help her assess those responses and tell her which guys were on the straight and narrow, and which, if any, were stringing her along.

Ashley readily agreed, and I think you'll find the results of our little experiment quite useful. Throughout each chapter in this book we'll discuss the various signs of deception, which ones (if any) these four gents used that night, and how Ashley witnessed them, whether she was paying attention to them or not. By the end of this book, you too will know which of these four men were lying (but not until the next-to-last chapter), and, just as importantly, how to avoid that same deception in the future by spotting it right away.

So, without further ado, let's meet our cast of characters and play our very own home version of that classic dating game, "Can You Spot the Liar?"

Ashley

Ashley is 30-something, professionally employed, attractive, well-dressed, and alert; everything you'd want (and need) in a Dating Detective in training. On the night in question, she showed up to a locally sponsored speed-dating event at a classy restaurant that had shut down on this Monday night to cater to busy singles looking for love in all the fast places.

She wore one of her favorite outfits, showed up a little early, ordered herself a glass of wine, filled out the appropriate paperwork, and took her seat at a cozy booth for two. A waitress came by with a number and taped it to the corner of her table, wishing her a cheery "Good luck!"

Ashley fortified herself with another sip of wine and looked at the two questions I had prepared for her that night. She had expressed to me that it seemed as though every guy she had dated eventually cheated on her. She was committed to finding a guy who had never cheated, and, what's more, who found cheating to be an unforgivable offense.

So I personalized the questions for her unique situation and came up with the following two queries:

- **Question #1**: *Have you ever cheated on anyone?*
- **Question #2**: *What do you think a woman should do if she finds out her man cheated?*

Each of these questions was specifically designed to elicit deception, if someone were so inclined. Just as importantly as *what* to ask, I had also coached Ashley on *how* to ask each question: not in order, not right away, and rather casually, throughout the meet-and-greet and interspersed through each conversation.

Ashley studied the questions until she had them memorized, put the index card I'd given her back in her purse, and then looked up to find the restaurant quickly filling up with members of both sexes.

As an overactive announcer addressed the group, livened them up with a few off-color jokes, and then stated the rules of the event—no physical contact, men should leave the table immediately when the buzzer goes off, and so on—Ashley studied the men milling about the bar waiting for the first signal to start the speed-dating event.

Most were, similar to her, young and well-dressed. They looked professional, polite, nervous, well-groomed, and alert. None of them seemed likely to be deceptive, and, for a brief instant, she wondered if that wasn't the whole point.

If a liar *looked* like a liar, she surmised, he wouldn't be very good at it, would he? Soon the speed-dating event was underway, and Ashley was being introduced to her first date of the night: Dave.

Dave

The night is starting out all right, thought Ashley as Dave walked up and broke the first rule of the event by shaking her hand before sitting down. His grip was firm but just right—masculine but not macho—and she warmed to him immediately. Dave was tall, dark, handsome, well-dressed, and sincere as he complimented her on the blouse she was wearing and asked if she'd just had her hair done.

Ashley resisted the impulse to swoon. Dave was her type, all right—the kind of guy she always fell for and was eventually cheated on, then dumped by. She tried not to hold it against him, and Dave made it easy; from the other side of the booth he practically oozed charm.

Ashley was careful to make casual small talk and enjoy the give and take of talking to her first speed dater. Dave was in business for himself. "Computers," he said cryptically before smiling and admitting, "Actually, I started a home repair company for computers three years ago and it's been going great ever since, mainly because I charge about half what Best Buy would to come out to your house and do the job myself."

Ashley was impressed with Dave's self-confidence and poise. Finally, with time running out, Ashley braced herself and asked Question #1: "Dave, have you ever cheated on anyone?"

Dave smiled, uncrossed his legs, and sat forward. "What do *you* think?" he asked cockily before snorting and saying, "Seriously, don't you think that's a little personal? I mean, I guess it would depend on what you mean by cheating."

Ashley shrugged in reply and admitted, coyly, "Fair enough, Dave. But let me ask you this," then she launched into Question #2 by asking, "What do you think a woman should do if she finds out her man cheated?"

Dave re-crossed his legs and hemmed a little before responding. "It depends on exactly what happened," he finally said. "I mean, I guess it depends on whether he comes clean. Did the guy apologize? Did he make it up to you? Who am I to judge?"

Ashley began to say, "Well, I'm not asking you to judge anyone, Dave, I'm asking you to be honest with yourself—" and the buzzer rang. As if they'd been talking about the weather, Dave leapt up and shook her hand again.

"I hope to be hearing from you soon," Dave said.

Despite herself, Ashley blushed and admitted, if only to herself, that he probably would.

Chuck

Ashley's next speed dater, Chuck, was in his late 30s but boyish-looking, with a baby face, wire-rimmed glasses, and a permanent smile. Although not as physically attractive or outwardly magnetic as Dave, he seemed sincere and his enthusiasm was contagious.

He, too, was a rule-breaker, shaking her hand immediately before sitting down. His hand was warm and clammy, Ashley noted, but, far from being grossed out, she thought it slightly endearing that someone who looked so outwardly confident could be so nervous on the inside. In no time they were laughing conspiratorially at some of the other, more blatantly desperate speed daters.

Chuck made all the right moves: He asked her about herself, seemed to listen while she talked, and even laughed at her corny jokes. Although she didn't exactly feel thunderbolts of physical attraction for Chuck, he certainly was easy to talk to, so it was no big deal for her to slip in our first question about a third of the way through their time together: "Have you ever cheated on anyone, Chuck?"

"No, absolutely not, never," Chuck answered immediately without so much as batting an eye. Looking her in the eye, he was very sincere as he queried, "Why do you ask?" Before she had a chance to answer, he concluded with a distasteful look on his face, "I have no respect for men who cheat."

Ashley wasn't quite sure if he'd answered too quickly, too perfectly, or if he was just being sincere. Intrigued, Ashley quickly followed up with Question #2: "What do you think a woman should do if she finds out her man cheated?"

Chuck hemmed for a fraction of a second before replying, "Dump him!"

"Ashley," said Chuck after an awkward moment of silence, "I have a confession to make...."

Uh oh, Ashley thought, *here it comes.*

But she was surprised when, instead of dropping the "I cheated on my last girlfriend" bomb on her, Chuck confessed to something else altogether: "I'm sorry I snapped at you," he apologized, although Ashley would hardly call being adamant about not cheating on someone snapping at her. "It's just, my last girlfriend? Well, to be honest, we didn't part on the best of terms. After dating for three years I found out she'd been unfaithful to me for nearly two of them, and, as understanding as I can be, sometimes to a fault, or so my friends tell me, that was just something I couldn't abide by...."

Despite her best friend's instructions not to nurture anybody there tonight, Ashley spent the rest of their time together doing just that. By the time Chuck got up, reluctantly, to move on, it felt as though they'd known each other for months, if not years.

She, too, was sorry to see Chuck go.

Phil

Especially when his replacement showed up! As he walked over to Ashley's table about halfway through the evening, she could see that Phil had "accountant" written all over him, from his polished black shoes to his gray, ill-fitting suit to his foggy spectacles to his business-cut, thinning hair. He seemed nervous and shy, and, out of the men she met that night, was one of the few who didn't break the rules by shaking her hand!

But, Ashley decided, she kind of liked that. She'd had her share of "bad boys" in the past (the Daves of this world), and was due for a rule-keeper by now. Phil didn't volunteer a lot; he kept quiet until asked something by Ashley. When she finally asked our first question, he seemed taken aback.

"Are you seriously asking me that? Do I look like that type of guy?" he asked, shifting slightly in his chair and sounding a bit defensive. "I mean, I don't see why that matters; I would never cheat on you!"

Ashley was impressed with Phil's vehemence. For a mousy-looking guy, he sure had passionate feelings about infidelity. Was that because, similar to poor Chuck, he'd been cheated on in the past? Or had he been the one doing the cheating? Ashley couldn't quite tell. The only way to find out was to forge ahead with Question #2: "What do you think a woman should do if she finds out her man cheated?"

"Let me ask you this," Phil countered, sitting up, "what would *you* do if you found out *your* man had cheated?"

"I *have* found that out, Phil," she confessed, eyes downcast, "and I wish I could say I broke up with him, but instead I forgave him and gave him a second chance. Instead of shaping up, he was unfaithful a second time. At least, I hope it was only two times! Either way, I eventually had to break up with him."

Ashley wasn't too sure about a guy who answered one question with another question of his own, but after her sobering confession, that didn't stop her from asking him a few more about his dating habits. To her surprise, he seemed open and honest and all too eager to get to know her better. (Maybe opening up had been his cue to do the same?) Unfortunately, Ashley wasn't sure she felt the same about good old Phil. (And, yes, he was in accounting!)

Sam

Ashley's last speed date of the night, Sam, was a tad on the young side, in his late 20s and dressing it to the hilt in skinny jeans and a simple, if clean, hooded sweatshirt. His face was unshaven and scruffy, but, she decided, purposefully so; his eyebrows were carefully sculpted and his eyes a deep, rich green. Despite the age difference, Ashley warmed to Sam immediately as he sat down across from her and made himself comfortable by leaning back in his chair and crossing his feet at the ankles.

The two made polite small talk for a few minutes until Sam's cell phone rang, but before he could embarrassedly silence it, she noticed his ring-tone was also one of her favorite songs. That brought up a lively discussion of favorite musical groups that lasted so long she only had a few minutes left when she finally thought to ask Question #1: "Have you ever cheated on anyone?"

Sam looked amused, sitting very still as he smirked and said, "No, not really. I mean, okay, on prom night my date got drunk and kissed two—no, wait, three—other guys on the dance floor, so, to retaliate, I kissed the principal on the cheek. Does that count?"

Ashley had barely finished laughing when she finally popped out Question #2: "What do you think a woman should do if she finds out her man cheated?"

This time, Sam was slightly more adamant. "She should break up with him; definitely dump him!" he said. "Absolutely, she should find a new guy!"

Watching Ashley nod in agreement Sam added perceptively, "Hey, is that why you're here tonight?"

Can You Spot the Liar?

So there you have it: four likely candidates and two very simple but ultimately revealing questions. Do you think you already know who the liar was—or who the liars were? Think the sniveling accountant with the foggy glasses had something to hide?

Think Dave was too charming? Or did you take him at face value and find yourself as charmed as Ashley had been? Think Sam was too honest for his own good, or that cuddly, cozy Chuck was able to make the night all about him without Ashley ever realizing it?

Don't be too sure. Sometimes the charmer really is charming and the bumblers really are just bumbling. On the other hand, you and I both know the popular saying: *If it seems too good to be true, it probably is.*

Maybe Dave's good looks are hiding a master manipulator. Maybe Chuck's good guy act really *is* just an act. Perhaps Sam is far beyond his years when it comes to manipulation, and who knows what Phil is hiding behind those foggy glasses of his?

I can tell you from experience that liars come in all shapes and sizes, and if you've ever been deceived by someone who just "couldn't, wouldn't, *ever* do that to you," you're likely to agree with me.

Of course, unlike Ashley, I wasn't paying attention to Dave's dark hair, blue eyes, or manicured fingernails; I was more concerned with how he was sitting when he answered Ashley's first question, how his voice changed, if it did, and what he said—or did—afterward.

The way Sam sat across from Ashley, to me, was far more interesting than what the ironic slogan on his hooded sweatshirt was, and, specifically, whether he was able to hold that relaxed posture when he answered Ashley's question, or if he shifted, just so, once he finally spoke.

As you will soon find out, it's not always what the deceiver says but what he *does* that points to deception. If it all seems confusing to you now, well, keep reading; your very own Dating Detective badge awaits!

Action Plan for Chapter 1

I want you to get to know our four speed-daters—Dave, Chuck, Phil, and Sam—a little better because you're going to be hearing from them later on in this book. So let's start a scorecard for each "player" and see how they stack up, deception-wise.

Read back through this first chapter and pay close attention to what you noticed as signs of possible verbal or nonverbal deceptions. Then, bookmark these pages in your book. As we move forward through each chapter and uncover more and more clues about who did and who didn't deceive Ashley that night, you'll want to keep score for your own edification.

FREE BONUS: Go to *www.lyingbook.com/bonuses* and download a digital scorecard that includes the action steps for this chapter.

EXCITING BONUS: Go to *www.facelessliar.com* and get your free excerpt of Dan Crum's new e-book, *The Faceless Liar: Is He Lying to You on the Phone, E-Mail, Text, or Chat?*

CHAPTER 2

Why Is He Lying?

Did you know that a lie is never just a lie?

In fact, there are several types of lies men can tell, various levels of deception, and even different reasons for lying. Some lies are classified as **deletion** (leaving something out of the answer for various reasons), others as outright **fallacies** (purposefully making a false or misleading statement).

Levels of lies include **significant**, such as lying about one's age, income, housing, or even marital status; and **harmless**, such as fibbing about one's weight, height, or IQ, say, in an online dating profile.

Have you ever wondered *why* men lie? You might be surprised to learn that not every lie is harmful or specifically designed to hurt you. In fact, some lies are more about protecting the men—or at least their strong sense of self—than they are about hurting or even affecting you.

For instance, a man might be lying to save himself from embarrassment (such as saying he's got a 36-inch

41

waist on his online dating profile when he's clearly a 38-incher creeping up on 40 inches when you finally meet in person).

Then, too, he might be lying out of courtesy to you (for example, not being absolutely forthright about what he really thinks about your new haircut or dress); he might even be lying to maintain his privacy (such as not giving you the full name of his multimillion-dollar company because he's been burned by gold-digging stalkers in the past or not letting you know what type of car he drives).

It's very important when learning to detect deception that you understand not just the **types of lies** men might tell you but also the **different levels of lying** there are and the **reasons for why men might lie** in the first place.

Understanding why men lie is key to detecting deception and will help you become a better Dating Detective. When you know that a man is lying to spare your feelings, for instance, it may not make you respect him more, but it might not make you trust him less. This is opposed to, say, when a man makes an outright false statement designed simply to deceive you, such as giving you the wrong phone number or e-mail address.

The following describes the various types and levels of lies, and reasons a man might lie.

The Two Types of Lies Men Tell:
Deletion and Fallacy

Let's say that on her speed-dating adventures, Ashley meets two new guys throughout the course of the evening:

"Leo" and "Chad." Both end up deceiving her, but each in his own unique and very specific way.

Let's start with Leo.

Leo wasn't what you'd consider a smooth talker, but because Ashley is now consciously looking to spot deception, she was wary of his nervous patter all the same, assuming he was hiding something.

When she asked Leo, "What do you do for a living?" for instance, he quickly responded, "I'm in securities." Ashley was impressed; she was no finance major but knew enough about Wall Street to realize that "securities" was some type of financial term. She dug a little deeper and asked where he worked.

Leo replied, "Downtown," and left it at that. Ashley brightened and said, "Oh, me too. I work in the Quincy building. Do you work anywhere near there?"

Leo mumbled, "Not far," but before Ashley could pursue the line of questioning any further, he quickly steered the conversation back to her. Though distracted, Ashley couldn't put her finger on when, exactly, Leo had deceived her, or how, let alone why.

Before she could put her finger on the deception, Leo's time was up, and Chad quickly sat down. Chad was youngish, vaguely hip-looking, and athletic. His skin was pale but firm and he hadn't shaven in a few days, making him look slightly more edgy than the rest of the middle-aged guys milling around in their khaki slacks and button-down Oxford shirts.

They exchanged small talk, and, eventually, Ashley asked about Chad's family. She was tired of feeling as though she was interrogating these guys, sick of hearing about boring accounting jobs, and just wanted to make a little small talk. Ashley herself was from a large family, and the way Chad talked it sounded as though he might be too.

"I've got a *lot* of brothers and sisters," Chad said enthusiastically after Ashley told him she came from a big family.

Feeling an instant connection, Ashley asked, "How many?"

Chad immediately said, "Two brothers and four sisters. Can you believe it?"

Ashley was impressed. "Four sisters?" she asked. "No wonder you have such good manners."

Chad politely blushed and the conversation moved onto the usual: work, weather, and so on. Just before he left, though, and seeming distracted after so much small talk, Chad was saying goodbye when he announced, "Say hello to your brothers for me. I always wanted a brother...."

Ashley shook her head, watching him go, a smile frozen on her face as she realized she'd just been blatantly deceived. Either Chad had lied when he told her he had two brothers, or when he'd just told her he'd always wanted a brother. Which was it, and, more importantly, *why* did Chad lie to her?

Why, indeed. Turns out both Leo *and* Chad had deceived Ashley, just in slightly different ways.

Deletion: The Art of Leaving Something Out

When Leo purposefully avoided answering Ashley's questions fully, by not telling her what, exactly, he did, for what company, or even in what building, he was engaging in a deceptive act known as deletion.

When someone deletes, information is left out for the purpose of deceiving you. Men who delete may not be lying to hurt you or purposefully deceive you; they just have a very strong belief that the less information you have, the better.

This may be because they were hurt badly in their last relationship because they over-shared, or got too close, too soon in a previous relationship. It may be because they were raised in untrusting households, or work in areas where information is power, such as in politics, the law, or even, yes, securities.

Men who delete information when responding to your questions, even minor details you would barely notice, believe that if you have all the information about them you will take a different action, such as reject or ignore them, or look at them differently, perhaps without respect or with less respect.

For instance, when Leo deleted information about what he did and where he worked, it wasn't because he was purposefully trying to hurt Ashley or even specifically "trick" or "fool" her; he was simply trying to look better in her eyes. His way of doing that was through deception—specifically, through not giving her all the information to fully, or truthfully, answer her question.

When Leo said he worked in "securities," it was actually to cover up the fact that he worked in *security*, as in "security guard." If Leo had told Ashley who he *really* worked for, Sutherland Security Corporation, she might have realized that he wasn't a financial planner at all but a security guard instead. And because the Sutherland

Security building was a local landmark around town, even letting her know the building he worked in would have given him away.

Why did Leo deceive Ashley in the first place?

Maybe he'd been looked down upon in the past by women who did not take his job very seriously, or maybe he was insecure about it for some reason, or maybe he was simply a private person who didn't want to share such personal (according to him) information with Ashley on their first meet-and-greet.

Some men are more comfortable with deception than others, and on the grand scale of deceiving people, men who delete don't score very high. In fact, Leo actually seems fairly uncomfortable deleting information with Ashley; he even leaves himself an "out" should they meet again and he was discovered, saying he's "in securities," which he can always go back to and explain, "What I meant to say was that I'm in *security*...."

Fallacy: Purposeful Falsehoods

We may never know which of Chad's statements was deceptive—that he already had two brothers or that he'd always wanted a brother. Either way, Chad had engaged in a type of deception known as a fallacy; in other words, an outright falsehood.

Synonyms for *fallacy* include a "misleading notion," an "erroneous belief," and even a "myth," so there's no hiding the fact that those who perpetrate fallacies are more than aware that they are deceiving you.

When men respond to your questions with a fallacy, they are saying something that's incorrect. Chad says he has two brothers, then he says he always wished he had a brother. Which is correct? The number of brothers Chad may or may not have is rather pointless to someone like Ashley, or at least should be, when seen in the light that whichever one is correct, the other is incorrect, and not just incorrect but **purposefully false**.

Again, not every man who replies with a fallacy is trying to hurt you, but more so than with men who merely delete, they *are* actively trying to deceive you. They may not even realize they're doing it; some men lie out of habit because they've been doing it so long. The longer they get away with it, the easier it is to do, and until someone calls them on it, they feel no repercussions.

The Two Levels of Deception:
Significant and Harmless

When men are being deceptive, they do so in one of two ways: Either their deceptions are **significant** or they are **harmless**. Significant lies have the power to harm, betray, and scare, whereas harmless deceit can still maim or wound in its own unique way.

Either way, you are being deceived, but the degree of deception varies.

Significant

- "I've only had three or four serious relationships in my life."

- "I make $250,000 a year."
- "No way; I'm not married!"

Such statements might not sound like deception at first. After all, many men prefer to be monogamous and not sleep around, millions of men earn a quarter of a million dollars a year, and many millions more are, in fact, single.

However, if a man has had many more than four serious relationships in his life and is downplaying that number, and if he doesn't make or hasn't made close to $250,000 a year, and, absolutely, if he *is* married, such statements are not only deceptive but *significantly* deceptive.

A deception is considered significant when it has the power to change your entire perception of a man. For instance, a person who makes less than $100,000 a year is no better or worse than someone who makes a quarter of a million dollars per year, but he *is* a very different individual.

If you are planning a life with such a man, your perception of him will be irrevocably altered upon learning of the deception. Perhaps you were looking to stay at home and raise children with this man; that may be nearly impossible to do at his actual salary, but quite easy to accomplish with his deceptive salary.

In other words, the deception is significant because it creates an entirely different perception of the man than if he had told the truth. On the other hand, a deception is considered harmless (on a relative scale) when the deception is so blatant or insignificant as to not drastically alter your perception of the person deceiving you.

Harmless

- "My other car is a Ferrari."
- "No way, only losers still live with their parents after 20."
- "I filmed an episode of *Entourage* last week."

Many men tell relatively "harmless" lies on a regular basis, without malice in their hearts. We live in a culture of haves and have-nots, of rich and poor, famous and not famous; there is very little in between anymore.

When men feel powerless, unsatisfied, less than special, or unattractive to the opposite sex, they naturally want to feel more powerful and more self-satisfied and make themselves appear more special and/or attractive, and they frequently do so by what I call "padding their emotional resume."

Men who tell relatively harmless lies figure, *Hey, everybody else is doing it, why shouldn't I?* It doesn't help that on the various online dating profiles and mate-matching services, it's almost expected that women will fudge certain aspects of their physical appearance while men are almost expected to add a few grand to their annual earnings, as well as inches to their height.

Why is it significant for a man to deceive you by saying he makes $250,000 a year instead of $75,000 a year, and harmless for him to say his "other car" is a Ferrari when he showed up to the date in a Honda?

The difference is in your own realistic expectations. $250,000 is a very specific number, and, in many occupations, a very realistic one as well. It's neither incredible nor fantastic to hear that a man makes that much a year. However, very few men drive a Ferrari, and most women assume that if a man says something such as "my other car is a Ferrari," he is either joking or trying to impress you.

As such, both are relatively harmless on the overall scale of deception.

The Four Reasons Why Men Deceive

Everybody lies, but not always for the same reason. Some men are out to hurt you, and that is why they lie; others are out to protect your feelings, and that is why they lie. There are plenty of reasons why men lie, and it's not always because they're bad people.

Following are the four main reasons why men lie.

Preservation: Double the Trouble

For decades men have been reared to be the provider, the alpha male, the worker bee, the sensitive soul, the defender, and the success story all rolled up into one. Now more than ever, with women competing in the same workforce and current economic conditions putting a strain on traditional family values as well as gender roles at home and in the workplace, some men are feeling threatened by their (perceived) lack of apparent success.

In the eyes of these men, five figures or even six figures just doesn't cut it anymore; they're "in it to win it" and when failure or a financial plateau inevitably comes their way, rather than being self-deprecating about it or giving themselves a break, they stubbornly cling to this successful, powerful, presentable image they've created for themselves.

For these men, deception is not necessarily about hurting you, but protecting themselves, or, specifically, protecting this image they've created for themselves. They want desperately to be perceived in a certain way, to be that successful, rich, creative, intelligent, handsome, fit, athletic, macho, sensitive, and so on, and, regardless of what image they are trying to create, what's more important to them is that you buy into it. Hence, their answers are all designed to support and reflect this carefully crafted image.

Specifically, there are two ways this image-conscious man will use deception to his benefit:

Self-preservation. When a man's sense of self is so important to him that he'll go to nearly any length to protect it, deception is merely part of his standard operating procedure. Men who respond deceptively in this category are doing so as much to support themselves as they are to deceive you. For instance, a man who has lost his self-confidence but whose very existence depends on success, money, and other confidence-builders will answer deceptively about his car, his current state of housing, his job, and his income to assure himself that his lies will soon become the truth as much as to cloud the truth to you. He may even likely believe this, and consider his deception "harmless" because even though he's only making five figures now, he'll soon be making six figures again, driving a nice car again, and living on his own (as opposed to in his parents' basement) again. This type of man believes you have to "fake it 'til you make it."

Image-protection. Self-preservation is the safeguarding of one's own sense of self, one's own purpose or place on this planet. Image-protection, on the other hand, is the act of preserving one's sense of purpose or place to others. So, for instance, a man might tell you he's "buying a new estate" when, in fact, he's downsizing because he has a certain image to keep up. Maybe he was in real estate and got used to the high times before the market bottomed out; he's now ill-equipped to face the bad times, and even though his finances are in freefall he just can't seem to let go of that image he used to have of being a high-flying, free-spending property broker. When he uses deception in this case, it's not so much to hurt you as it is to impress you.

Courtesy: Your Feelings Matter to Him

We are brought up to believe that all lying is bad, or, if not necessarily bad (depending on the scruples meter in your home while you were growing up), then at least done to hurt you. But did you know that there was a specific type of deception designed to actually help spare your feelings?

Maybe you've asked a male coworker, "Do you like my new dress?" And maybe he's immediately answered, "Absolutely," even when it's not really all that flattering. Perhaps you've asked, "Do you like my new haircut?"

after sitting down with a date in a crowded restaurant. And maybe he's instantly replied, "Yes," even when he doesn't.

This is not to say that the dress wasn't smokin' and the haircut wasn't stunning, but most men are taught that unless the dress is ridiculous and is going to ruin a woman's reputation for the rest of her days, or a haircut is so atrocious she might be attacked by birds upon leaving her house in the morning, we are supposed to say "yes," "great," "fantastic," "super," or some other pleasantly rewarding superlative upon being asked about such matters.

Is this deception? Technically speaking, yes. If a man feels your dress is less than flattering but tells you otherwise, he is, in the strictest sense, deceiving you, but he is doing so to spare your feelings.

Privacy: Why So Personal?

- "How much do you make a year?"
- "How's your sex life lately?"
- "What kind of car do you drive?"

Now, admit it—these are fairly personal questions to ask a man on a blind date, a first date, or even a third date! Maybe it's in your personality to be curious; maybe some guys respond to that and have nothing to hide—or lots and lots of confidence. Some men, however, balk at such personal questions; they see them not as fun, funky, whimsical chit-chat, but as more of an interrogation, perhaps even an investigation. In short, they take them personally.

Rather than saying, "Hey, that's personal," or "None of your business, lady," men like this will instead deceive you to protect their privacy. They won't shy away from the questions. In fact, they may even embrace them, but they'll be doing so deceptively.

For instance, if you ask in passing how much this type of man makes, he might say, "Six figures," despite the fact that he only makes $50,000 a year. Or he might say "I haven't had a serious, intimate relationship in a while," but lately he's been hooking up with more women than Tiger Woods on a trip to Vegas. He might even point to a red-hot sports car in the parking lot and call it his own, even though it's a rental, or his brother's, or his dad's!

In this case, the deception isn't necessarily to make the man look better, as it was in the case of self-preservation or image-protection, but instead to keep some privacy to himself.

Maybe they'll say they make six figures when, in fact, it's many times more than that; they simply want you to like them for them, and not the big, fat wallet they're sitting on. Maybe they won't tell you what kind of car they drive or point to the correct one, because they don't want you writing down the license plate number while they're using the men's room (hey, it happens). It's a privacy issue for them; nothing more, nothing less.

Now more than ever, we live in a world of self-protection and barriers. Women are trained, nearly from birth, not to give out their phone numbers and/ or addresses to strange men, to keep a distance, to not rush into things, to remain private and aloof until trust in a relationship is sufficiently manufactured.

Men, too, are increasingly interested in making sure they have some barriers, and fudging on a few discreet answers on a date, or even a job interview, is a good way to throw up those barriers.

Deception: Plain and Simple

Last but not least, the fourth reason men lie is, quite simply, to be deceitful; to deceive you, plain and simple. This is outright deception; there's no other word for it. It may or may not be malicious, with ill or harmful intent, but this type of deception is a flat-out lie.

For instance, a married man might say, "What? That pale strip on my ring finger? Oh, I cut it last week and it had a band-aid on it while I did work in the yard all day." This is neither deletion nor fallacy, and it's much more significant than harmless; this guy is flat-out lying to you, and the sooner you spot the lie, the sooner you can quit wasting time trying to date him.

Or a job candidate might say, "I'm currently unemployed," when, in fact, he's working for your biggest competitor. He might even say he already has his MBA when he's actually several credits away from graduating. Although he may *almost* have his MBA, and that would have been good enough for you, he didn't say that; he said he already has it. That's deception.

A car mechanic might say, "You need an all-new brake system, front and back, and it's going to cost you $1,700," when, in fact, all you need is brake pads that a friend could install for $120, parts and labor combined.

We know that men lie for a variety of reasons; we also know there are different degrees of deception. What we can't deny is that a lie is a lie, regardless of the reason, and that the worst kind is a flat-out, plain-and-simple, old-fashioned, bold-faced lie.

Action Plan for Chapter 2

Now that you know *why* men lie, it's important to start categorizing the various forms of deception you may hear in a given day. For instance, you've seen in this chapter alone the two main forms of deceit:

- **Deletion:** Leaving something out.
- **Fallacy:** Purposefully lying outright.

As you begin looking out for deception in your life, don't just generalize it by saying, "Oh, I think this guy is lying to me." Get specific; determine if a man is hemming and hawing and deleting information in order to be deceptive or if he is just flat-out issuing a fallacy—in other words, straight-up lying to you.

What I suggest is to keep a running tab every week. (It can be a little depressing thinking people are lying to you every day!) But if, on your way to work every Monday, you remember to stick a scrap sheet of paper in your purse, briefcase, laptop bag, or backpack, you can use one side to list all the deletions you hear, and, on the other, mark down how many outright fallacies you hear.

It's easy to lose track of just how often we are deceived at any given time. When you actively begin to keep track of not just when you suspect deception, but which type of deception you suspect, this Dating

Detective stuff becomes much more real to you. Also, as you get a better grip on the distinction between deletion and fallacy, you can also start determining which types of lies men tell: significant or harmless.

A typical entry might read something similar to this:
Tuesday afternoon. Brent deleted that he'd run into his ex-girlfriend while at the mall. Significant.

Thursday night. Alan "forgot" that he'd already told me he was going to a rock concert Saturday night and said he was going to his mother's birthday party instead. Fallacy—significant. Sunday morning. Tyler forgot to mention he'd gotten a speeding ticket on the way to my house the night before. Deletion—harmless.

Remember, the goal is not to add up all the deceptions and reflect on how evil men are; the goal with this exercise is to specifically categorize and label deception so that you are not only aware that you are being lied to, but also how, why, when, and where.

FREE BONUS: Go to *www.lyingbook.com/bonuses* and download a digital journal that includes the action steps for this chapter.

EXCITING BONUS: Go to *www.facelessliar.com* and get your free excerpt of Dan Crum's new e-book, *The Faceless Liar: Is He Lying to You on the Phone, E-Mail, Text, or Chat?*

CHAPTER 3

Don't Look for Truthful Behavior

Have you ever gone into a movie just knowing you're going to love it?

Maybe you're a big fan of the director; you love all her movies and really respect what she's done with her profession. Or maybe you've got a crush on the lead actor, have followed his career, and know he's a dependable professional. Maybe it's an adaptation of your favorite book, and you know that this director, with this material, can do no wrong. Or perhaps you're just really in the mood for a cozy English mystery and this one has all the right elements going for it.

In short, you are predisposed to enjoy this film. For whatever reason—director, actor, adaptation, genre—all the cylinders are firing in this love connection on film. Forget what the critics say, forget that it's not the director's finest work, or that the lead actor has a horrible British accent, or that they butchered the book, or that it was neither cozy nor a mystery; chances are you're still going to feel warm and fuzzy when you leave the theater.

59

Why? Because you had a preconceived notion going into the movie that you were going to love it. You didn't reserve judgment, didn't rank the movie on its merit, didn't judge the performances, didn't get objective; you just sat there in that theater and enjoyed it.

Ladies, I hate to break it to you, but *this is what you do with men*.

You are predisposed to believe what they say, biased against distrusting them, and actively looking for truthful behavior because it's what you want. And it's what you expect, because *you're* telling the truth, and, darn it, so should they. In other words, you are using your preconceived notions about men, or a certain type of man, to "frame" everything they do or say.

Don't Put Your Men in a Frame

One of the biggest problems with being deceived is that we actively look for truthful behavior, and during that search we often tend to ignore occasionally obvious or at least telltale signs of untruthful behavior.

Case in point: If I trust my dad and know he would never lie to me, I have a bias of him as an "honest guy" and I would naturally *frame* all our conversations to trust everything he says and notice what I feel is truthful behavior.

Framing is something we do subconsciously; it's part of the subconscious bias we have (more on bias in our next chapter) such that our preconceived notions about a person, a type of person, or even a group of people, color our judgment and allow us to distrust when it's not necessary and be deceived when we're trusting instead.

It's called *framing* because you put the person in a box, a frame, where he or she exists in a small vacuum of your own creation. The outside world ceases to exist; inside the frame is where all the action is.

Unfortunately, *you* have designed the frame, not the potential deceiver.

So naturally, everything he says exists in, gets filtered through, and is viewed within this frame of your own design. It's like that movie you loved so much despite the fact that no one else could stand it; you had framed that motion picture within your own preconceived notions to the point at which no one and nothing—not even the movie itself—was going to stop you from enjoying it.

Men are the same way; if you look for truthful behavior you are going to find it. If you look for him to tell the truth, if you interpret all the signals he's sending based on your own criteria and not by listening or reacting to what is actually being said and/or done, then you're going to find truthful behavior whether it exists or not.

In this chapter I want to teach you the very important principle that says you should never look for truthful behavior. Why?

It's simple.

Truthful Behavior Can Be Faked

If you look for truthful behavior, you are actually helping the man give you what you want; you are actually giving any and every man 50 percent of the equation he needs to deceive you. And if your man is any good at deceiving you at all, he's got the other 50 percent in his pocket.

Your contribution to the equation makes his part easy; because you're already looking for truthful behavior, he only has to try half as hard to deceive you! And what's his 50 percent of the equation? Simple. He has learned in time to fake truthful behavior so that between you looking for it and him faking it, you will see truthful behavior—oftentimes whether it's there or not!

Deceptive men don't just start with you; you're not their first time at the rodeo. Many deceptive men have been getting better and better at being deceptive by deceiving more and more women throughout a longer period of time. A guy can tell his little story over and over again, and on each date he refines it a little more, fine tunes it just a hair, until he's basically a mini master of deception. Perfect practice makes perfect.

How does he refine it? He watches carefully for your and every other woman's reaction when he tells his stories. So if he's bragging about his yacht and all the celebrities he had on board this weekend and mentions a particular A-list star's name and a woman rolls her eyes in disbelief, he knows instantly he's gone too far—and immediately starts improvising for the next telling of the story.

It's too late to pull it back on this one; the mood is broken, and he's likely been caught, but the next time, instead of dropping George Clooney or Colin Farrell's name, maybe he mentions someone a little more believable, say, Carrot Top or Pauly Shore—they're still celebrities, they still have that name recognition factor going for them, but, more importantly, they're both much, much more believable.

Details are a deceptive man's stock in trade; the fewer details he has to remember, the better. And the more reliable, consistent, and similar the details are every time, the fewer opportunities he has to screw up. So rather than switching from a 44-foot yacht to a 23-foot yacht to something else, he's going to want to keep his story straight.

Now he's refining his patter so that it's the same size yacht every time; it's the same celebrity every time; it's the same exotic destination, the same pheasant under glass for dinner, the same expensive brand of champagne, and so on. Like the best craftsmen of lies or inventor of stories worth telling, he keeps what works and uses it over and over, throws out what doesn't, and replaces it with something that *will* work.

Once he's got his story down pat, he knows just when to tell it, how to tell it, what points to sell, what words to emphasize, and when to pull back. Just like any other performer, the deceiver becomes an expert at mimicking emotions to fake truthful behavior.

In fact, anybody who has studied up on what psychologists, talk-show hosts, doctors, and best-selling authors consider "the signs of truthful behavior" or practiced them effectively can fake truth; it's actually quite easy.

How do you get around this obvious behavior?

It's simple: *Stop looking for truthful behavior*.

What is truthful behavior? There are basically four kinds of truthful behavior:

- Sincerity.
- Eye contact.
- Verbal and nonverbal consistency.
- Straightforward answers.

Sincerity

When Bill Clinton lied on national television about not sleeping with "that woman," his former intern Monica Lewinsky, the country bought it—at least for a while. Why? Because Clinton had learned to master the appearance of sincerity.

Clinton was such a master that many of us believed him as long as we could—until the evidence was so strong there was nothing else to do but consider ourselves deceived.

As Clinton and so many smooth-talking deceivers prove, sincerity is actually quite simple to fake, particularly when you are looking for truthful behavior, such as sincerity. Sincerity, *true* sincerity, has a string of descriptive synonyms, to include *genuineness, honesty, naturalness, authenticity,* and *earnestness.*

In other words, when someone is sincere he or she is being the opposite of deceptive. Unfortunately, sincerity is one of the easiest human emotions to fake because it is marked by several expressions, attitudes, or postures, which deceptive men will actually practice for full effect.

Many people are fooled by an easy smile, but there are actually two kinds of smiles: sincere and insincere. What's the difference? A sincere smile reaches the eyes; it creeps up past the nose, over the cheeks, illuminates the eyes, and forces crow's feet or laugh lines to appear because it is an obvious, instantaneous, and sincere gesture.

Conversely, insincere smiles don't reach the eyes; not even close. Instead, they kind of stop at the nose. Deceptive men are smiling to evoke in you an emotion such as, "Oh, he's happy so this must be going really well," or "Oh, he's smiling so I'm doing fine...." The more at ease you feel, the more likely you are to look for truthful behavior and ignore the warning signs of deception.

Emotions can also be sincere or insincere. For instance, if a man asks you how your day went and you say your cat died, the practiced deceiver will instantly see this as an opportunity to appear sincere and so will automatically respond with something such as, "Oh, you poor thing. Are you sure you want to stay out? Would you rather be home grieving?"

A sincere man might say the same exact thing, *but* he would also follow up on it. He might share a story of a childhood pet that died, ask you about your favorite memories of your cat, offer condolences, or offer to cut the night short.

It's very confusing when a man fakes sincerity, because he is often so good at it that you can't tell the real thing from the wrong thing. One way to tell is that true sincerity has follow-through. A sincere person won't just pay lip service to your dead cat, your lost job, your fight with your roommate, or any other problem you might be having; he will follow through, listen to you vent, and offer comforting words that aren't just platitudes designed to console you and move on with it.

Insincere men, on the other hand, don't know how to respond to genuine human emotion so they'll often try to move you away from it as quickly as possible. There is no follow-through because they aren't sincere in their concern. They really can't follow through because they just can't understand why this matters so much to you.

Why? Simple: because it matters so very little to them.

Finally, posture can be a simple way to affect sincerity. For instance, if he's leaning over when you speak, that's showing you he can listen and be attentive. If he's careful to pull out your chair, order your drink first, hand you your drink, pass over the bowl of nuts, and so on, such posturing is contrived to evoke sincerity.

This is not to say he's not being sincere; many men are and have been raised with manners that affect these postures in a sincere way. But it is easy and effective for the deceiver when he practices sincerity, and he can fake it without detection.

Eye Contact Does *Not* Mean a Staring Contest

One of the biggest signs of sincerity is **eye contact**, but the deceiver often mistakes eye contact for a staring contest. I realize all too well how easy it is to do! Ever since I heard about formal eye contact in my first days of CIA training, I simply cannot have a conversation with someone without engaging in formal eye contact. I just don't want people to think I'm not being sincere when I'm talking to them.

After all, looking someone in the eye is one of the easiest ways to convey sincerity; deceivers know this. They know that women appreciate eye contact, that they're on the lookout for it, and that all the self-help books about dating tell you to look for it. Deceptive men know that if they can somehow fake eye contact, they can easily convince you that they're for real.

But it's uncomfortable when two people have intense eye contact all the time; it's like a staring contest. Genuine sincerity, conversation, and human interaction should feel and look natural. It's not forced or practiced, rehearsed or carefully orchestrated.

Most people will break eye contact from time to time—not to deceive you, but to be natural. Maybe something catches their eye across the room, the waitress has just appeared with your drink order, or they feel as though they've been staring at you.

Deceivers don't know when to naturally break eye contact for personal comfort; they assume that because people look for eye contact as sincerity, they should simply do it almost all the time—regardless of how it feels for you or them.

What *is* the appropriate amount of eye contact? In general, the standard rule for appropriate eye contact is seven seconds on, three seconds off. In other words, it should feel comfortable, natural, and normal to keep eye contact with someone for seven seconds or so before it starts to feel uncomfortable.

Typically, you then look away, blink, or the like, for up to 3 seconds before looking that person in the eye again for another 7 or so seconds, and so on. Not that you need to keep a stopwatch handy or tick off "one

one-thousand, two one-thousand," but you will get a feel for this type of normal eye contact as you go along.

Verbal and Nonverbal Consistency

The third kind of truthful behavior is something I call **verbal and nonverbal consistency**. In other words, a person's words should match what his body is doing; this should be a natural, not unnatural, verbal and physical expression.

So if a man says that he's relaxed but he's obviously uptight, tense, and "clenched," physically speaking, this is *not* verbal and nonverbal consistency; this is, in fact, verbal and nonverbal *inconsistency*.

In its simplest form, verbal and nonverbal consistency occurs when the mouth and the body match up, when they align and don't cause you obvious and apparent concern. When you say no and mean it, you shake your head; when you say yes and mean it, you nod. Deceptive people, however, say no and nod their head. Why? Because they don't mean it.

If you say to a man, "Are you going on any other blind dates this weekend?" and he immediately says no even when his head is vaguely nodding, this is inconsistent.

Truthful behavior appears to be a consistency between verbal and nonverbal behaviors; it will appear sincere because it matches up. "Yes" equals a nod, and "no" equals a shake, not a patchwork, inconsistent equation.

Straightforward Answers to Straightforward Questions

Nothing should send the alarm bells ringing in your head more than when you ask a simple question and get a convoluted, twisting, TMI (Too Much Information) answer. Honest people react honestly, with simplicity.

In polygraph testing, we spend a lot of time making sure that all test questions can be set up in a way that the answer is very direct—always as a yes-or-no answer. The way to ensure honesty in a response is to begin with straightforward questions that require simple answers.

Remember, I am not trying to turn you into a full-fledged interrogator, and we don't want you to treat every pleasant evening out like a scene straight out of *Dragnet* ("Just the facts, sir").

Men have different personalities and respond differently to different questions. Some men get nervous and rattle off 10-minute answers to a 10-second question; others respond in clipped tones because they can't catch their breath. There are many reasons a man might yammer, stammer, stutter, or stump you in the first few minutes of a blind- or first-date scenario.

However, by the time you've spent a few minutes together, the pressure should be off, the drinks should have arrived, the nerves should be far less jangly, and things should return to normal. That's when a man's response rate should be how they usually respond when they're at their natural best.

So as you're meeting and greeting, remember to save the more probing questions for later on in the evening, at least until you're 10 to 15 minutes into the date. This may not be possible in a frantic party or speed-dating scenario, of course, but then neither case is ideal for really getting to know someone. However, when you *do* ask a simple question, look for a simple answer. What is a simple answer? One that is direct and straightforward, effortless, and to the point.

Let's say you ask a man, "Seen any good movies lately?"

Now, most guys would light up and say something like, "Actually, I don't know what kind of movies you're into but *Avatar* is really good. I'd see it again with you, if you're up for that kind of thing."

This is far from a yes-or-no answer, but we're also far from a polygraph room. This answer is simple ("*Avatar*"), direct ("is really good"), straightforward ("I'd see it again with you"), and clear ("if you're up for that kind of thing").

Now, ask a deceptive man the same question and the response could be quite different. "No, all the movies are really crappy lately. I used to see a lot of movies with my last girlfriend, and even though we broke up months ago, she'll still call me from time to time and invite me to one. Like, she called last week—out of the blue, I mean, we hadn't seen each other in days—and asked me to go to that new *Transformers* flick? I told her we were still broken up and no way could I go see it with her...."

Now, you don't have to be an expert in covert surveillance or hardcore espionage to see the writing on *that* particular answer's wall. I mean, this is *not* an answer about movies; this is an answer about some past relationship that still sounds fairly current.

In fact, this guy sounds downright defensive, pointing out in various ways and at various times that he's *not* still seeing her (even though he says he'd seen her a few days ago), she *never* calls (even though she just did), and that *no way* would he go see a movie with her, ever (even though it sounds like he maybe could have, just by accident).

These might be two fairly obvious examples, but sometimes life can be just as obvious. When you stop looking for truthful behavior, the sound of deception can be quite deafening.

Now, I'm not saying that everyone who gives long-winded answers is necessarily deceptive; some people just like the sound of their own voice or actually have lots to say. But when you ask a direct question ("So, seen any good movies lately?"), you should expect and be watchful for a straightforward answer ("Absolutely; *Avatar* rocked!")

Don't Look for Truthful Behavior: In Review

So let's review what we have covered so far. Don't put your men in a frame, because everything they say or do will get filtered by the frame you created. We all have biases that affect our ability to give people a fair chance in communication. We also tend to look for truthful behavior, which limits our ability to identify deception. The biggest reason we don't look for truthful behavior is because truthful behavior can be faked.

To overcome these challenges you need to consistently use our favorite phrase, which is: Get REELL. (Read the next chapter for more.) With this clear and fresh approach, you can communicate with people and improve your ability to identify deception the majority of the time.

Action Plan for Chapter 3

On a slip of paper or in your journal, list the four kinds of truthful behavior:

- Sincerity.
- Eye contact.
- Verbal and nonverbal consistency.
- Straightforward answers.

Keep the list handy: at your desk, on your fridge, by your bed, in your bathroom. As you review your conversations each day, keep a running tally next to each type. For instance, if you were genuinely struck by three sincere behaviors that day, write a "3" next to #1: Sincerity. If you experienced deep, genuine, and moving eye contact twice that day, write a "2" next to #2: Eye contact. And so on.

This exercise will help you get a feel for trusting your intuition. It's important to recognize that truth exists far more often than deception. However, we're not here to actively look for truthful behavior, so there is naturally a second component to this exercise. Now, next to the number you wrote for each type of truthful behavior, write a minus sign (-). Next to that, write the number of times you felt someone was *insincere* to you that day.

So, for instance, if the smarmy guy in sales made a big deal about your "new outfit" even when it was something you know he'd seen six times already and he was clearly being insincere, write a "-1" next to #1: Sincerity.

Or if someone was really intense with his eye contact and it felt awkward, put that next to the minus sign; do the same for numbers 3 and 4 as well. So, to the right of each type of truthful behavior you should have an equation: "3 - 1 = 2" or "4 - 3 = 1," and so on.

As you complete this exercise each day, you will start to get a better feel for truthful versus untruthful, sincere versus insincere, and so on. This will give you a leg up as you continue toward your honorary Dating Detective degree!

FREE BONUS: Go to *www.lyingbook.com/bonuses* and download a digital journal that includes the action steps for this chapter.

EXCITING BONUS: Go to *www.facelessliar.com* and get your free excerpt of Dan Crum's new e-book, *The Faceless Liar: Is He Lying to You on the Phone, E-Mail, Text, or Chat?*

CHAPTER 4

Get REELL

When people learn of my CIA background, they often wonder how I was able to leave the job behind when each day's shift was over. They immediately assumed that just because I was trained by, working for, and had experience with the Central Intelligence Agency, I constantly went around interrogating everybody I knew, be it consciously or subconsciously, personal or professional.

I'll admit it wasn't always an easy transition from polygraphing a prospective CIA officer to, say, having dinner with my wife, lunch with a good buddy, or a round of golf with friends.

When we finally understand the capacity for human deceit, it's easy to see it everywhere, even in the harmless day-to-day "white lies" and "deletions" of close family and friends. Other times we go in the opposite direction, giving certain people a "pass" on deceit because of how they look, how they are related to us, how long we've known them, or because of their background.

We do this subconsciously, labeling whole groups of people with a predetermined bias, and eventually letting that bias (which we'll talk about shortly) determine not only how we feel about that person but also how we interpret what they do and say.

Now that we know *why* men lie, it's time to start getting in the mindset of actually detecting deception so that we're finally able to do something about it. This chapter provides one of the most useful tools you'll need to detect deception, and, the best part of all, you already have the two requirements necessary for putting this tool to work: your eyes and your ears.

Now, remember, the goal of this book is not to make you paranoid about people lying to you all the time or to create a deep distrust of men. There are many, many good men out there who are not out to hurt you, would never even think of deceiving you, and, in fact, look forward to creating a rich, rewarding, and romantic life with you.

> Do you want to meet and marry your soulmate? Do you want to find that love that can last a lifetime? You need the Soulmate Success System by Dan Crum. Go to *www.abcsoulmate.com* to learn more.

The trick is in knowing when to be on the lookout for deception and when to relax and go with the moment. This chapter provides you with a tool to help you "reset" the subconscious but deeply ingrained preconceived notions you have about people, so you can view them without blinders on.

Address Your Bias Focus and Take Off Your Dating Blinders

Before we get down, get dirty, and Get REELL, I would like to talk for a few moments about why it's so important to reset our minds and approach each inter-action without our "dating blinders" on. What are these dating blinders? They are the preconceived notions, the minor and major biases we have about people before they even open their mouths.

You see, our minds are pre-programmed to make assumptions about people based on a variety of factors: sex, height, weight, race, salary, eye color, hair color—you name it, we've developed a preconceived notion about a person within several seconds of meeting him or her.

This is a very bad habit and one that we all share. In fact, this is such a bad habit that it even has a name: **bias focus**. Now, some people call it a prejudice, but I know none of you are prejudiced, so we'll stick with "bias focus." Our bias is that we generalize groups of people as being or acting a certain way.

Let me give you an example. Complete this sen-tence: "All men are_____!"

I'm going to guess that most of you gave the same answer, but it doesn't really matter what that answer was, just that it came to you automatically. These auto-matic thoughts, these immediate and instant reactions, are just one symptom of our bias; we don't even need to think about men anymore to immediately categorize, label, and prejudge this specific group. (Not that some of us don't deserve it!)

We don't always believe such a statement as fact, but it is so deeply, habitually ingrained in our minds that this predetermined bias affects the way we communicate with men.

You see, when we have a bias, we alter our perception of a situation and tend to frame it to meet our bias, regardless of what the individual is really saying, really doing, or, for that matter, is really like.

For instance, if you answered, "All men are pigs," well, that is definitely going to color your perception of every single man you meet, regardless of any and all evidence to the contrary. If you feel that all men are pigs, then when you walk into a man's office and see papers scattered all over his desk, you immediately have framed the scene as "this guy is messy and unorganized." In short, it's just another piece of evidence that yes, in fact, all men really *are* pigs.

Now, if you ask him what he is doing and he tells you he is working on an important project on a tight deadline and his desk doesn't normally look that way, well, regardless of how logical an answer that is, you will *still* tend to judge his response based on your original bias.

In short, you will tend *not* to believe him rather than fight your bias and give him the benefit of the doubt. Because your bias has programmed you to think all men are pigs, and this man certainly seems to fit the bill, what he actually says is less important than your predetermined notion of this man before you even met.

Now complete *this* sentence: "All women are ____." (Hmm, not so easy this time, is it?) Let's say your answer was "All women are great multitaskers." Now, when we enter the office of a woman with papers scattered all over her desk, you have immediately framed the scene in your biased mind as, "Well, obviously this woman must be very busy, or maybe she is organizing her paperwork."

There is simply no other explanation, thanks to your bias. So now when you ask her what she is doing and she tells you she is working on an important project, you judge that response based on your bias. Clearly, this frazzled and overworked woman is working under a tight deadline!

In both situations, your bias had a direct effect on your ability to judge fairly whether you believed the answer to your question. To be outstanding at identifying deception the majority of the time and to trust that your perception is accurate, you need to fight your bias; you need to give everyone a fair chance, no mater what that individual has done in the past.

"Get Real!"

Have you ever been confessing something even *you* know is foolish to a friend, a partner, a coworker, or a loved one, and he or she stopped you, looked you dead in the eye, and told you to "Get real!"?

Maybe you were telling them that the reason your new boyfriend didn't have a job and had to keep borrowing money was because he was overqualified for everything. Perhaps you were sharing with your friend that the real reason your boyfriend kept answering the cell phone and walking away to talk to people whenever he was around was because he was an international art dealer and didn't want any of his rich and famous clients to hear you giggling. Whatever the reason, when someone tells you to "get real," it's usually because they're hearing the truth behind your statements—even when you can't.

"Get real!" is one of those "snap out of it" sayings that instantly reminds us that what we're saying—or in many cases, hearing—is pure malarkey, 100-percent wishful thinking.

"Get real!" is what you say to the used-car salesman when he tells you the beat-up old junker he's trying to sell you has only been driven by one little old lady.

"Get real!" is what you say to the cheating boyfriend who just crept inside the bedroom window with lipstick all over his collar and phone numbers sticking out of his pockets, when he tells you he was out late volunteering at the local homeless shelter.

But what do you say to yourself when you suspect a man is deceiving you?

What do you say to yourself when you want to believe him, but know you shouldn't?

What do you say to yourself when your BS meter goes off the charts, but your first instinct is to ignore it?

I'll tell you what you say: You say, "Get REELL."

Get REELL

"Get REELL" is more than just a clever acronym or great way to remind you to realign your bias focus when meeting someone new. Instead, Get REELL is a mindset; a kind of reset button you can hit every time you encounter a situation in which you have a preconceived notion about someone: a work interview, for instance, a blind date, buying a used car, or when your little brother calls and you know he's going to give you some excuse as to why you should lend him another $50.

When you Get REELL, you enter a place where you're not judging, just observing; it's called a mindset because you're working actively to disengage from your bias focus and see what's beyond your preconceived notion about this man for whatever reason.

For instance, if you are biased against used-car salesmen, you are not going to believe *anything* a used-car salesman tells you. Even if he's being honest and trying to get you a great deal on an affordable car that has good gas mileage and a new A/C system, you're still going to distrust him regardless of his words or actions. In short, you turn off your eyes and ears and become a slave to this bias focus of yours. This is one case in which your bias makes you distrust someone who was actually trying hard to earn your trust by being honest.

Bias works the other way too. Perhaps you are too trusting of guys who remind you of other guys. Let's say you've always had a thing for tall, gangly, curly haired, bookish types with a great sense of humor. This is your personal "relationship kryptonite," and you're nearly powerless against this type of guy's particular charms.

So naturally whenever you meet a guy like this, you are predisposed to trust him. He might be the biggest player, hustler, con man, and creep in town, but your bias is so strong it's going to take him doing or saying something completely, obviously untrue for you to *not* trust him. So here is a case in which your bias subconsciously allows you to trust someone who is being quite deceptive.

When you Get REELL, you don't automatically find a lie, and you don't immediately trust or distrust, but you instantly put yourself in a better position to find a lie because you are open to both honesty and deception.

In other words, Get REELL is a place you can go before a blind date, before a job interview, before buying a used car, or before talking to your little brother, where you're still you, still your old bubbly self, just more aware, more in tune, and more prepared to detect deception when and if you come across it, because you're ignoring your bias focus and focusing instead on what your eyes and ears are telling you.

When we're biased or preconceived to trust or distrust someone, we let our emotional baggage and stubbornness decide for us whether or not someone deserves to be trusted. When we Get REELL we rely not on emotions or the past but instead on the factual evidence our eyes and ears are giving us.

The "REELL" in Get REELL stands for:

- Reset.
- Eyes.
- Ears.
- Look.
- Listen.

Leave Your Emotional Baggage at Home and Treat Each Date Like a Blank Slate

Have you ever heard of the thought process that says you can't expect to get different results unless you take new actions? Meaning, if you keep doing what you've always been doing you will keep getting the same results you've always gotten.

If you keep getting deceived, it's not because you're a bad or "slow" person, or that you deserve to be deceived; it's simply because you keep doing the same things over and over again so that nothing ever changes. In short, you keep distrusting that used-car salesman even when he's telling the truth, and blithely trusting that tall, gangly charmer even when he's selling you a bill of goods.

You simply can't keep hearing the same fibs, half-truths, deceptions, and complete untruths over and over again and think someone is going to stop telling them to you unless you demand to stop being lied to in the first place.

Instead, change your bias focus, and reset your preconceived notions so that you approach each meeting with a blank slate, and use your eyes and ears to look and listen so that you can decide for yourself, based on the evidence, whether a man is deceiving you or not.

What you need is a choice; you need something to help you detect deception so that you can take the power back from the deceiver. You don't have to choose between going out and getting deceived; you can make wiser, more rewarding choices when you have better information.

By knowing the Get REELL system, you now have a choice. You can choose to *not* Get REELL and keep being deceived, or you can Get REELL and determine when, in fact, you are being deceived, and then *do something about it*.

In other words, you can choose whether you want to try these principles using the same approach, looking and listening to things the same way, or you can choose to Get REELL, and, by resetting your eyes and ears and looking and listening from a fresh perspective, you can finally get new results.

"Get"

Now, before we delve further into the REELL aspect of Get REELL, I want to remind you that this is a mindset you need to "Get" into. Until you practice it often, it doesn't happen automatically. You have to work at it, as with everything else in life that's worthwhile, so that eventually you learn to Get REELL wherever, whenever, and with whomever you need to.

So the "Get" portion of this helpful little acronym is a kind of mental speed bump to remind yourself to slow down, put on the brakes, open your eyes and your ears, and focus on what a person is really telling you, not what you think about him—subconsciously and most likely without merit—simply because he's bald, short, rich, or poor, or drove up on a bicycle in a sweater three years out of fashion.

The "Get" speed bump reminds you that, yes, you have biases against men and that, no, they don't always apply to every man, every time.

"Get" is what you do before you use the REELL terms to **R**eset your **E**yes and **E**ars, **L**ook, and **L**isten. In life we have little triggers we have to learn to avoid so that they don't set us off. Sometimes that trigger is alcohol, or cigarettes, or food. Let's take food, for instance.

If food is our trigger, say sweets or chips or ice cream or coffee cake, we can't put ourselves in the path of temptation and expect to escape unscathed 100 percent of the time. The more we expose ourselves to triggers without forethought, the more our diet is going to unravel. So we weigh ourselves, budget our calories, and carefully avoid tempting situations. If you know that Chinese buffets are kryptonite to your diet, before you go into one you slow down, form a plan, and stick to it.

You don't willy-nilly load your plate, but instead you prepare yourself as you pick up your plate and carefully pile it up with fresh steamed veggies and brown rice before adding a little protein in the form of steamed chicken or beef. You don't deny yourself completely; you don't treat it as a prison sentence; you just "Get" prepared so that you don't ruin all the hard dieting work you've done all week.

Well, when you Get REELL, you also prepare yourself to avoid temptation—the temptation to give into your bias focus, the temptation to judge without reason, the temptation to believe any old thing you're told, the temptation to be fooled, and the temptation to trust when no reason to trust exists.

Reset

If "Get" is the speed bump that tells you to slow down and let go of your unconscious bias, then "Reset" is the stop sign that says to throw your bias out the door and prepare a blank slate for your next date, interview, or business meeting. Why do we need to reset our minds before a blind date, a job interview, a big negotiation, buying a used car, or any other scenario in which we might possibly be deceived?

We need to reset our way of thinking because our day-to-day mindset is wired in such a way that we let bias rule our rationale, and anything that clouds our judgment or makes us assume someone is either deceiving us or being truthful based on what we think versus the evidence they give us will eventually make us susceptible to deception.

Let's say your bias focus tells you that all men with thinning hair, big guts, and glasses are harmless. You don't consciously repeat this mantra every morning, but it's there in the back of your head nonetheless, so that your defenses go into red alert when a scruffy guy in peg jeans and a motorcycle jacket sits down across from you, and you go into safe and secure mode when Mr. Baldy shows up.

Trusting or distrusting a man based on his appearance is a clear case of bias and can get you into trouble when you start believing everything Mr. Baldy says and distrusting everything Mr. Biker says.

So when we switch to "Reset" mode we don't automatically become distrustful of everyone and anyone we meet, nor do we do the opposite. Instead, we reboot, or reset our deception-detecting system to reserve judgment until all the evidence is in.

If you've ever seen a Tom Clancy flick, a James Bond film, or one of the *Bourne* movies, it's a little like when the super spy puts on his night-vision goggles; nothing about the spy changes, and nothing about what the spy is looking at changes; only *how* the spy sees the bad guy changes.

What was invisible to him before he put on his night goggles is suddenly clear.

Getting into "Reset" mode is like putting on your "deception-vision" glasses. It won't change you, necessarily; it certainly won't change who you're talking to. It won't change what you order to drink, what he wears on your date, or even what he says during your date.

Getting into "Reset" mode will, however, *change how you view* what he says, because it helps you abandon your bias focus for a four-part system that helps you use your **E**yes and **E**ars to **L**ook and **L**isten.

Eyes

Too often we ignore what we see when we're on the lookout for deception. We think we should see very obvious signs when someone is lying to us, such as beads of sweat on his brow, averted eyes, trembling hands, or fidgeting feet. But, as we've learned so far in this book, some men can look you straight in the eye and lie with a smile on their face the entire time, whereas others won't look you in the eye even when they're telling you the 100-percent truth.

In future chapters I'll tell you very specifically what to look for to spot deception. To Get REELL, though, you just need to know how important it is *to* look, for now, rather than what, specifically, to look *for*.

Your eyes are the gateway to your senses; they are the front line a deceiver must cross before he can even begin to lie. If a guy can get past this first line of defense, if he can pass muster visibly, then half the battle is already won. When it comes to detecting deception, it all starts with the eyes. That's why the first thing you do after resetting your senses and becoming aware of your surroundings is to first use your eyes to assess the situation.

What is he wearing? What did he drive up in? Who got there first? How does he treat the hostess? The server? What does he order? Does he order for you first? How is he acting? Nervous, confident, scared, assured? Where are his hands positioned? His feet? Does he show any emotional ticks when he's talking to you? Is he meeting your eyes or avoiding them? Is he too intense? Too laid back?

For right now it's not as important to interpret what you see, as it is to be on the lookout for anything and everything, and that, immediately after entering reset mode, you begin to process any meeting with your eyes first. It may seem too obvious to say this, but you have to consciously open your eyes to deception to see it.

Ears

If the eyes are the gateway to your senses, then the ears are the guardrails! The ears help you support what you see, keeping you on track as you continually assess the situation for deception. In the CIA we had a saying: "Don't believe what you see until your ears agree."

In other words, a guy can look like a complete and utter creep and yet tell the truth 100 percent of the time. Likewise, he can come off like the cover of a romance novel while every word coming out of his mouth is absolutely, positively deceitful.

The ears are more than just a backup system when your eyes fail you; they act more like a team member, working in concert with your eyes. That is why it is "Eyes" *and* "Ears," "Look" *and* "Listen," and not just one or the other; you really *do* have to use both senses to detect deception; one sense alone just isn't enough.

Let's say you're on a job interview, and before you actually sit down for the Q & A, the representative from human resources takes you on a tour of the department you'd be working in. Now, despite the HR rep's smiling face and polished demeanor and what he's telling you about your new job, what you're seeing is a whole other story.

People look overworked, unfriendly, and stressed, and your eyes are telling you that what you're hearing about "team spirit" and "departmental harmony" simply isn't accurate. It may not be downright deception when he says "working for this department is a real team effort," but it's certainly not jibing with what you're seeing.

Likewise, let's say you're on a blind date, and, because you're ready to Get REELL, you show up early, find a seat near the window, and put yourself in a "Reset" frame of mind. As you do so, you notice your date pull up in a sleek black sports car that really gets your engine racing. Yet after some polite conversation, when you ask him what he drives, he tells you that "material things don't matter to him," that "getting from A to B" is what really counts, and that he drives "an old car just to get around."

Or maybe he wants to impress the "green" side of you so he says he drives a hybrid when you clearly saw him pull up in a gas-guzzling sports car. Or perhaps what kind of car he drove up in doesn't matter because when you ask he says he came by taxi.

Why he says these things is immaterial at this point; he is being deceptive. What *is* important is that you Got REELL. You didn't just listen to what he was saying— you looked *and* listened; you didn't just believe what you saw, but waited to hear what he had to say before making a firm assessment.

Look

Now, unfortunately, just seeing and hearing aren't enough to Get REELL. You can see something and not believe it, not interpret it, not register it, not absorb it; the same goes for your ears. So with the first three components of Get REELL, you first Reset your mindset to prepare to use your Eyes and Ears more effectively. This is a great starting point; now with the last two letters you're ready to actually "Look" and "Listen," and suddenly you're entering all new territory.

When you see something, it has no value unless you interpret it with experience, forethought, and knowledge. A splattered piece of canvas may look all but worthless until you hang it on a museum wall and find out it's actually a Jackson Pollock painting; then everything changes. One kid out of 100 on a busy schoolyard playground looks just like any other until you spot the one that's your little brother; then everything changes.

Clues to deception are like that: They have very little meaning if you're only observing them without understanding them. You must learn to interpret them as well. So merely seeing and hearing have little value to you unless you get active about interpreting them. For instance, let's say that during the course of a blind date, the gentleman stays mum on his personal habits. In other words, he doesn't come out and say he drinks or smokes too much, but all the evidence is there if you'll only look for it.

So it's 6 p.m. and all starts well. You order a white wine spritzer and he orders a vodka and tonic. That's fine, that's entirely cool. You sip your wine spritzer and he downs his cocktail, quickly ordering another. By the time you've finished your first drink, he's had three. Maybe he's nervous, you think...until, after two more stiff drinks, he's barely feeling the effects. So that's five drinks in and he's barely tipsy. This tells you, if you're paying attention, seeing *and* looking, witnessing *and* interpreting, that you could be dealing with a heavy drinker.

And maybe while you're watching him toss back those drinks you notice that he has a familiar-looking, cigarette box–shaped bulge in his jacket pocket, and a tendency to use the restroom frequently and come back smelling of smoke. So even without asking a single question you can tell this guy knows his way around a cocktail party and smokes.

Is it deception?

Not necessarily; not until he speaks—then you have to **listen** and decide for yourself.

Listen

Just as seeing is the twin sense to the ears, listening is the twin tool to deception-detecting. You simply *have* to listen to what someone is saying and interpret it, much the same way you interpret what you see. If a guy says he doesn't drink...listen and observe. If a guy says he doesn't smoke...listen and observe.

- What is he really saying?
- What is he really doing?
- Do his words match his actions?
- Do his actions match his words?

In later chapters we will learn what men are really saying when they move their lips. I promise you'll find it fascinating, revealing, and, most of all, useful. But what you don't use can't help you, so first we really have to get you in the mindset of realizing the vital importance of listening to what a man says and applying it to a rigid interpretation.

Citing the previous example, let's say you've clearly witnessed someone who knows his way around a bar and obviously smokes. This is seeing, this is looking, this is observation—and it's absolutely vital in detecting deception.

But...the analysis is not complete until he's actually deceived you verbally, if and when you call him on it. For instance, let's say after five vodka and tonics in less than two hours you can't help but say something such as, "Tough day?"

Who knows? Maybe it really *has* been a tough day and he needs to unburden himself. Maybe he's just lost his job and would really like to open up and talk about it. This could be a breakthrough moment, a chance for him to really open up, and a chance for you to really get to know him. Or he could just have a drinking problem. Either way, this is a golden opportunity for you to find out—or a missed opportunity if you don't even try.

So what does he say when you inquire about his day, assuming that it's been a "tough" one? He says, a tad defensively, "Not really. Why do you ask?"

Being a good little Dating Detective, you mention the five drinks he finished, look pointedly at the fresh highball in his hand, and say, "Well, you really seem to be knocking them back tonight. I just assumed you'd had a tough day."

"Oh, that?" he says, waving off the other drinks while holding tight to his new drink. "That's nothing to worry about. You sound like my mother."

You appear concerned and say, "Well, it's just a lot for one person to drink in under two hours. I just thought, if you were upset, you might want to talk about it."

Now, by this time you've given him not just the benefit of the doubt but also every opportunity to (a) trust you and (b) respond to you truthfully. Instead he shrugs it off, or gets defensive, and says, "Naw, I just know how to handle my liquor." (As if you don't.)

Or maybe, after seeing the cigarette-shaped bulge in his jacket pocket, after watching him visit the bathroom four times in an hour and smelling the smoke on him each time he returns, you finally say, "I'm sorry if this sounds personal, but do you smoke?"

And let's say he answers very quickly, "No, why do you ask?"

And you point to the "evidence" in his coat pocket, remind him that he seems to go to the bathroom a lot, and that he always comes back smelling like smoke. Now, an honest person wouldn't have said no when the answer was yes, but because it's a blind date and he doesn't know you all that well, he may have simply omitted that fact—and fibbed to cover it up.

Caught, the average person would blush, hold out the pack of cigarettes, and *admit* that they were caught red-handed. Yes, he was originally deceptive, but remember what I said in a previous chapter about privacy issues—or even wanting to protect you?

Maybe he's just really, *really* insecure about his smoking, has tried a million times to quit, and really likes you and didn't want to disappoint you or cause you to shut him down on the spot simply because he smoked. If that's the case, his harmless deception is easily forgivable. (Remember, we're here to detect deception and use the results to make better decisions.)

Now, a deceptive person might further dig himself a hole by blowing the whole thing out of proportion, turning it around on you, and making you feel guilty for even questioning him in the first place—all the things poor Ashley went through during her speed dates in our opening chapter. The power of Getting REELL is that you refuse to feel guilty about asking a simple question. Embarrassed when you find out your assumption is wrong, maybe, but never guilty.

Of course, there's another option in this scenario: Maybe he really *doesn't* smoke. Maybe he smirks and pulls out a little box of chocolates from his jacket pocket and gives it to you as a gift, explains that he's nervous and that makes him go to the bathroom a lot, and, what's worse, the men's room is right next to the kitchen help's smoking section so he really can't avoid coming back smelling of smoke.

The great thing about listening, and the harmful thing about *not* listening, is that if you never *ask* the guy about it, *listen* to his responses, actively *interpret* them and decide for yourself whether he's being deceptive or not, you'll never be satisfied.

In short, when you Get REELL, the knowledge, the power, and the decision-making all shift back to you. You take the power away from the deceiver and give that power back to yourself so that you are now in control, not him.

Action Plan for Chapter 5

As a reminder, Get REELL stands for:

- Reset.
- Eyes.
- Ears.
- Look.
- Listen.

Print the letters on the back of your business card just as they appear here, or maybe on a sticky note or some other small reminder that can fit in the palm of your hand. (I like writing them on the back of a business card because it fits squarely in the palm of your hand and can be referred to often.)

Place the card, sticky note, or notepad where you can refer to it often—maybe in a front pocket, near your computer monitor at work, or in the top drawer of your desk. When you are socializing with people throughout the day—not just guys, but anyone—take it with you and refer to it often. Eventually you won't need the card or sticky note; you will remember what Get REELL stands for. But for now, just keep it handy so you don't have to guess.

As you enjoy a carefree lunch, as you're enjoying dinner with friends, or even on a date, refer to the Get REELL motto often. Get into the habit of "Resetting" so that you can use your "Eyes and Ears" to "Look and Listen."

You might be jazzed about the concept now and don't think you need to practice, but I think this process is so vital—and you will too when you read further—that I'd really like you to use this action plan to your advantage and cement the Get REELL acronym in your head.

Using the card, or eventually your memory, get into the habit of Getting REELL whenever you socialize. I'm not suggesting you interrogate your friends or grill every guy you meet, but I am suggesting that you practice the Get REELL philosophy so that when you do wind up in situations in which you need to **R**eset your **E**yes and **E**ars, **L**ook, and **L**isten, you will not only be prepared, but fluent in the process.

EXCITING BONUS: Go to *www.facelessliar.com* and get your free excerpt of Dan Crum's new e-book, *The Faceless Liar: Is He Lying to You on the Phone, E-Mail, Text, or Chat?*

CHAPTER 5

Your Window of Focus

When it comes to detecting deception, you can't do so in a vacuum. Everybody is different, everybody comes from different backgrounds, and everybody has formed different patterns of behavior that, to them, are perfectly normal. In other words, what looks like deception on Joe could be truthfulness in Jim, and vice versa.

Thanks to the movies and TV, everyone believes there will be some big "tell" when a person lies to them, like a nervous tick, an upward-right eye movement, or sweaty palms. But some people have a nervous tick when they talk, period, whether they're telling the truth or lying; some folks habitually look up and to the right because that's how they're hardwired; and, frankly, some guys just plain have sweaty palms.

This chapter will help you develop a "Window of Focus" you can use to tell if a man is deceiving you. Rather than being some long and involved process, your WOF is a rapid-blink reflex you will build in time that helps you take a five-second mental movie of how a man reacts to a specific question.

We'll delve into the entire process throughout this chapter, but for now, know that when you're through reading it, you will gain just one of many concrete techniques to help you detect deception in men. Best of all, there are only four simple steps to finding your Window of Focus:

- **Step #1:** Start with a WIN (What Is Normal).
- **Step #2:** Learn the four question types to determine deception.
- **Step #3:** Don't forget to Get REELL before asking relevant questions.
- **Step #4:** Find your Window of Focus.

Step #1: *Start with a WIN (What Is Normal)*

To tell whether a man is deceiving you, it is important to determine What Is Normal, or WIN. In other words, when this guy is just sitting around the house, being completely relaxed, carefree, and, above all, truthful, what is he like? Some people call this being at rest, others call it a man's default setting. It's how he behaves when he's basically just being himself.

Gregory Hartley and Maryann Karinch, coauthors of *I Can Read you Like a Book* (Career Press, 2007), call it baselining. "Baselining is a portable version of the polygraph," they write. "You use it to pick up subtle variables in body language and tone of voice. Once you know what to look and listen for, you can detect changes that accompany stress of varying degrees. That ability gives you a high degree of control in your interaction with someone."

Whether you call it being at rest, a default setting, or a baseline, your goal here is the same: look for his WIN, or What Is Normal. When you know a man's default, baseline, or "normal" setting, you can tell when he's responding *ab*normally to your questions. In other words, when you know how he acts at rest, you can notice how he reacts under stress.

Questions are what we call the stimulus to observing behavior and observing responses. Let me say that a different way: by asking people questions, you activate their autonomic nervous system to show you deception when it is happening.

Here's an example: Let's say you wanted to know whether a guy you were on a date with had ever had a one-night stand. This is the easy part—ask him, "So, have you ever had a one-night stand?" Trust me, this question will catch the guy off guard and his response will quickly and easily reveal whether or not he has.

The problem with such questions it that most women just stop there. They haven't figured out WIN yet so they have no idea how to determine deception based on the guy's answer. Just because a guy jumps out of his seat when you ask him if he's ever had a one-night stand doesn't mean he's lying when he says no, or telling the truth when he says yes. (It could be a false confession!) Many guys would jump out of their chairs at that question, particularly if it's coming out of left field, whether they've ever had a one-night stand or not!

So in order to judge how a man responds to your questions, you first have to figure out his WIN, or What

Is Normal. You can't detect stress if you don't know what normal looks like. By "normal" I don't mean whether the guy is weird or not. What *normal* means when detecting deception is, what is the guy's default setting, his baseline? How does he act when he's not under the lights, not being grilled, not being interrogated? (Not that you would ever do any of *those* things, of course!)

To start with a WIN and find out what "normal" is for the man in question, you can follow these simple steps.

Engage in Small Talk

Not every word in a conversation should be loaded; not every question should have meaning. Sometimes talk is just that—talk. When you engage in small talk, when your questions are light and your gestures and tone are nonthreatening, you put the man at ease so that not only can he relax, but you can also see how he acts, what he says, and how he gestures when he relaxes.

Remember, ideally the guy is at ease so that you can see what he's like normally. If he's on edge, tense, or always looking to defend or prove himself to you, you'll never know what he's like normally because you just won't see it.

This is bad for two reasons: one, if he's deceiving you, it's going to be harder to tell because you'll never see what he looks like in relaxed mode; and two, if he's *not* deceiving you, you're going to miss out on getting to know a potentially great guy.

During small talk, loaded, baited, or charged questions (more on them momentarily) are off limits. Right now, you're just chatting about simple, informal, casual things such as the weather, a local sports team, movies, music, interests, and hobbies. As you chat informally, look at how he's responding as he begins to relax, and ask yourself:

- Does he use his hands as he talks?
- Does he say certain phrases all the time, such as "all right," "great," or "sweet"?
- Does he say things such as "you know what I mean" or "honestly" when he talks?
- Does he cross and uncross his legs habitually?
- Does he stammer, stutter, or blink rapidly, even when just talking casually?

It's important to find out what he does all the time, even when he's relaxed—we call this **habitual behavior**—in order to spot when he breaks from this behavior while being questioned.

For instance, maybe he's a fidgeter; maybe he's just wired to be full of energy and it's hard for him to sit still, even when he's very casually chatting about what movies he's seen lately, his favorite sports team, or the weather. Knowing that he's a fidgeter—or a nail biter, or a sweater, or whatever—is going to help you avoid spotting false clues if and when he deceives you.

Let's say you ask him something a little more critical, such as, "So, have you ever had a one-night stand?" Well, if he fidgets when you asked him that question, it doesn't necessarily indicate deception because, after all, he fidgeted *before* you asked the question and will be fidgeting long *after* your date is through.

Small talk (light, casual topics that don't pose a threat) is a great way to Start With a WIN. Here are some general topics that will put your guy at ease:

- The weather.
- Sports.
- Hobbies.
- Work.
- Cars.
- Celebrities.
- Current events.
- Movies.
- Music.
- TV.

Ask Some Lay-up, Nonthreatening Questions

In basketball there are hard shots and there are easy shots. A three-pointer from half-court with the defense going crazy, the fans going wild, .01 second from the buzzer, and the game on the line—that's a hard shot. Going in for a simple lay-up right under the net with some pudgy, tired guys from work playing defense... well, that's relatively easy.

In this section I want you to shift from having some casual, nonconfrontational small talk to asking some nonthreatening, easy, lay-up questions. This will allow you to begin gradually introducing harder, tougher, or leading questions later, but for now, what you're still trying to do is get him to relax, get him mellow, smiling, laughing, and talking so that you can learn What Is Normal.

Samples of some nonthreatening, lay-up type questions include:

- "What was the last vacation you went on?"
- "What bands are in your favorite playlist on your iPod right now?"
- "Where did you go to school?"
- "Where did you grow up?"
- "How many brothers/sisters do you have?"

Look for Habitual Gestures and Movements

Now, during small talk, while you're getting him nice and relaxed, it's time to get to work looking for things the man does regularly and habitually.

Habitual gestures include those things we do without even thinking about it. Oftentimes such habits can go back to our childhoods, when we were very young. For instance, how do you put on your shoes in the morning?

Do you put your socks on both feet, then your shoes on both feet, then tie both shoes? Or do you put on one sock, one shoe, and tie that shoe before addressing the other naked foot and starting the (habitual) process all over again? Neither is right or wrong, but one or the other was probably taught to you as a child and you've been (habitually) doing it ever since.

If you stick your tongue out when you pay your bills, work a calculator, or type, chances are you were the kind of kid who stuck her tongue out when you colored in a worksheet in kindergarten or did your spelling test in 1st grade.

These gestures become habits because we do them so often, and after a while, we do them without even thinking. Therefore, it's extremely important to look for certain habitual gestures a man makes while he's relaxed so that you can discount them if and when he tries to deceive you. For instance:

- Does he pinch his ear every time he answers a question?
- Does he cross and uncross his legs?
- Does he look around the room when he's talking to you?
- Does he make eye contact?

Remember, none of these things *on their own* mean he's being deceptive, nor do they mean he's being truthful; they just mean he's being *himself*. And, right now, that's more important. The more you can see what he does while he's at rest, relaxed, and normal, the more information you have when things get a little more serious later on.

Listen for Qualifiers and Habitual Phrasing

Qualifiers are a tactic some people use to distance themselves from the truth. Sometimes they do this consciously by hedging their "bets" (answers), so to speak. Sometimes they do this out of habit, because they've always done it that way.

You hear qualifiers all day long; maybe you even use them when you speak. Qualifiers are words and phrases such as *sometimes, maybe, could be, to the best of my knowledge*, and so on.

The opposite of a qualifier is a definitive answer: *yes*, *no*, *every Tuesday*, *last Thursday at noon*, and the like.

When interviewing someone truthful he or she will often use fewer qualifiers and be more declarative. If I ask, "Do you drink?" and he or she is a non-drinker, instead of hemming and hawing, he or she will simply say no, or "Used to, but I quit six years ago," or "Does a glass of champagne on New Year's Eve count?"

Qualifiers are words that help a person avoid talking directly about something he might find uncomfortable, unsociable, or unseemly; he may also be hiding deception.

When you're trying to determine what's normal in a subject, you are not actively looking for deception; just the opposite. You want to see, hear, and feel how he acts when he's just being himself, at his default setting; what he's like when his guard is down, when you've put him at ease. So in this case we're not actively looking for conscious, sketchy, obvious qualifiers that hide deception, but those that he might use habitually, just because they've been a part of his speech pattern for so long.

For instance, there's a guy I know who says "typically" a lot; this is a habitual speech pattern for him. When it started I have no idea, but it's a constant in his speech.

For instance, I might ask, "How long will it take for this job to get done?"

He might say, "Typically, I can do this job in six weeks."

Or perhaps I'll ask, "Can you get to this over the weekend?"

And he might say, "Typically I don't work weekends, but in this case I should be able to get to it."

Although "typically" *is* a qualifier, in this case he's not being deceptive or cagey. I think he's just hedging his bets in case the job takes eight weeks instead of six or five; that way, by saying "six weeks," he's covered.

Another good example is when a salesperson or politician is taught to respond habitually to all questions by immediately responding with, "That's a good question." Take notice if you hear this response when determining WIN, because this type of response would be deceptive if it wasn't part of WIN.

It's important to look for habitual phrasing so that if you hear it when you actually start asking more serious questions, you won't mistake it for deceptive behavior.

Step #2: *Learn the Four Question Types to Determine Deception*

Now, once you've determined a man's WIN, you have a canvas on which to paint a series of questions designed to get the information you want. Without knowing What Is Normal, it would be difficult to know what is abnormal, so now you are much better prepared to ask these types of questions.

Also, these steps work in order, 1 through 4. So far you've learned how to gauge a man's normal, baseline, or default setting, which sets you up to learn the next step, which is the right kinds of questions to ask to determine that. Later in this chapter we will talk more specifically about the final step in the process:

your Window of Focus, that brief, five-second opportunity you have to detect deception based on all you've learned so far.

For now, though, here are the four types of questions I'll be teaching you to use during your Window of Focus.

Simple and Direct

Often we try to make our questions elaborate and multilayered in order to "slip in" the true question, or to try and throw up a smokescreen around the real issue we're trying to get at; these are called *indirect questions*. Men are very good at sniffing out these types of questions, and may be wired to respond deceptively, or at least indirectly, when posed with a multi-pronged question that requires multiple answers. Instead, the first types of questions I want to introduce are the kinds that are simple and direct. Simply put, direct questions usually require a simple answer. Not all will be yes-or-no, but all will have a definitive answer. For instance:

"Do you live alone?" requires a simple yes-or-no answer.

"When was the last time you spoke to your mother?" is not a yes-or-no question, but it can be answered simply, as in "Last night" or "Last month."

It is important to note that when you determine what questions to ask, you should try your best to ask simple and direct questions the majority of the time. The other question types will evolve from the creation of simple and direct questions.

Assumptive

Assumptive questions program an answer into the question by using an assumption as an actual part of the question. Assumptive questions can be leading in that they don't leave a lot of wiggle room for the respondent. Let's say you suspect that a guy you've been dating is unemployed. Maybe he says he goes to work every day, and yet four or five times a day, during the week and normal business hours, he's calling you from home. You might ask an assumptive question such as, "When did you get fired from your job?" The assumption here is that he is no longer working for the company he claims to, and by further assuming he was fired (a severe case versus quitting) you create an opportunity for the guy to acknowledge he no longer has the job, and save face by telling you it is because he quit for some justifiable reason (rather than being fired).

Negative

Negative questions force a man into a corner to take a stand, one way or another, about a negative situation. For instance, "Shouldn't you be drinking less if you're driving home?" is a negative question. He can only answer in one of two ways: defensively or truthfully. Another example is, "Isn't that girl over there checking you out?" You're not asking, "*Is* she flirting with you?" You're asking, "*Isn't* she flirting with you?" The distinction is that she *is* flirting with him, and he must either confirm or deny. One distinction to make is that when you ask a negative question, you should be attempting to influence your subject to do something or agree with you. Here is another example: You are scheduled to go to a mutual friend's home after your date and you really don't want to go. Instead of just asking your date if he wants to go, use a negative question such as, "You don't really want to go to that party, right?" This strategy makes this question type both negative and leading, and, most importantly, persuasive.

Baited

A "baited" question is the most manipulative of these four tactics. Baited questions introduce a potential scenario to your subject that forces him to consider whether that scenario may occur. As he considers the possibility that the scenario may happen, a guilty person will often "take the bait" and show their deception with an explanation for the scenario, whereas an innocent person is not concerned about the potential scenario. Most often, baited questions only come into play when you highly suspect a man of being deceptive or have actual proof of a specific issue you think you're being deceived about, such as your man is unemployed or cheating on you. In that case, a baited question might sound this way:

- "Am I going to get an e-mail telling me that you're still seeing your ex-girlfriend?"
- "When I send this e-vite, is your boss going to respond telling me you don't work there anymore?"

Step #3: Don't Forget to Get REELL Before Asking Relevant Questions

Step #3 reminds you to Get REELL, or Reset your Eyes and Ears, Look, and Listen, before you begin questioning to determine your Window of Focus. Getting into a nonjudgmental, unbiased mindset won't just protect the man from being unfairly judged, but will also protect you from judging unfairly.

We all want to be fair here—fair to you and fair to him. So much of this chapter has focused on treating the man fairly, as if he wasn't deceiving you. When you Get REELL, you also get rid of your bias against men in general, particularly certain types of men whom you think are deceiving you when they're actually not. Or vice versa—those whom you feel aren't deceiving you when they are.

What Is Normal, or WIN, applies to you as well; you need to establish a baseline or default setting such that you go into the date, interview, or relationship unbiased against or toward a certain individual so that you too are a blank slate and can base your decisions on what is actually happening versus your *perception* of what is happening.

The best time to Get REELL is right before you open your Window of Focus.

Step #4: Find Your Window of Focus

Your Window of Focus is a brief period of time during which you should be on high alert for signs of deception. In other words, there is a period after you ask a question and a man responds in which you should be highly aware and powerfully focused on his response.

Remember, it's not so much the question that requires your focus, or even the second or two it takes him to absorb it, but his actual verbal and nonverbal response.

Now, a Q & A with a Window of Focus has a very specific three-part format:

First, you ask the question. Remember, your Window of Focus does not open the second you ask the question.

Second, you give the man time to take in the question. Some men respond more slowly than others, so this process can take one to two seconds, depending on the man. So, first you ask the question, and then he takes it in and actually understands it.

Third, there is a response period. The moment he has taken in the question, your Window of Focus should open for a short time: only about five seconds after question-acknowledgement should you look and listen for signs of deception.

The Window of Focus is like that moment when you take a picture and light floods in and freezes the image on the film (or, in modern terms, on the memory stick). Opening your Window of Focus should start to become habitual, such as when you Get REELL; the more you do it, the more used to it you will be.

Why is the Window of Focus so important? Well, dates are distracting, men are exciting, conversation gets hectic, drinks are served, and maybe there's dinner and candlelight, wine and dancing. Even a neutral setting can become overwhelming when outside variables such as loud music or bad acoustics take over.

The Window of Focus will give you a clear mental movie of how your man reacts to a question no matter the setting, the time of day, the noise level of your surroundings, or the view.

It is your own personal video of how he responded physically and what he said to answer your question; by focusing on it, you can play it back again and again and analyze it thoroughly both during and after the question.

Here are some ways to enhance your Window of Focus so that your mental movie becomes clearer and clearer with each question as opposed to blurry and unfocused due to outside distractions:

Try to find an opening (a segue). Often we're in such a rush to get a burning question answered that we just go ahead and blurt it out at the most inopportune time. This is not the most effective way to open your Window of Focus or get a serious response. Guys go on high alert when women get anxious, and when an anxious woman blurts out a question, chances are your guy will shut down, whether he's telling the truth or not. So to ensure the best chance of eliciting a specific response, wait for a natural opening, pause, or segue in the conversation before asking your question.

Pipe down after you ask. So much of our conversational patterns overlap; we often start talking before the other person stops, interrupting each other with layers and layers of conversation that have no clear beginning, middle, or end. The best way to ensure a prompt and specific response from a man is to ask the question and then pipe down. Just listen. The key to an effective Window of Focus is taking that precious five seconds while the man is responding to your question to really, actively look and listen for deception. The quieter you are during those five seconds, the clearer your Window of Focus will be. Remember, if your question is simple and direct you have no need to ask the question again or clarify it. People tend to be afraid of silence or uncomfortable asking serious questions, and, as a result, you can taint your Window of Focus by talking before he answers or before he has said his piece.

Give him a second to take in the question. We've already established that this is the second part of your Window of Focus process, but it can't be stated enough: Don't start looking for deception while the man is taking in your question. Instead, give him those few seconds to absorb it and *then* zero in on his response. Usually this kind of "in-between" period is marked by a kind of blank stare, a passive "what next" expression, and a lack of real physical or verbal movement as the question sinks in; so really, it's not a great place to look for deception because it's just too soon to judge.

Look and Listen for signs of deception that start within five seconds of question recognition. Here is the real Window of Focus; here is where your job begins. If he's going to deceive you, throw you off the scent, or con you, it will happen within this very specific, very brief five-second Window of Focus. And that is why it is so important to know What Is Normal, because if you are going to be put off by every tick, stammer, leg cross, or "uhhm," your Window of Focus will be less than clear, and these habitual or default behaviors will throw you off your game quicker than you can say "I've been deceived."

Anything outside this window is usually not related to your question and should not be taken into consideration. The reason there is a specific *Window* of Focus is because you're looking *in* the window, not outside or around it. So what he does before you ask the question doesn't count in regard to this specific question, and what he does or says after he's answered the question and moved on also becomes irrelevant because the Window of Focus has passed. The one exception to this rule of looking and listening inside the window is when the deceptive words or actions started inside the window and continued beyond the five seconds. In that case you must consider all words and behavior as relevant until he stops talking or until his body comes to rest.

In the next chapter we will talk about the conscious and the subconscious, the visceral reactions people have when questioned and the more control they can spin on something once they've registered the shock. What happens in the Window of Focus is specific and measurable as it pertains to the question asked, and the reason the Window of Focus is so short is that after five seconds, the man can control his reaction or shock and color the results. But within that brief period of time his reaction is blunt, visceral, and often uncontrollable, meaning it's pure gold for those trying to detect deception.

Be careful not to pester or interrogate, or you may cause deception that appears legit. Imagine someone suspects you of stealing something from your coworker, and asks you, "Did you take something from John's office yesterday?" If you are innocent, your natural response will probably be, "No, what was taken?" Now imagine the accuser is not satisfied with your answer and starts to push you on this issue, basically interrogating you, as he or she continues to ask you more questions related to the theft. Innocent people actually tend to get more upset than guilty people when they have already claimed their innocence but are not believed. In an attempt to defend themselves they will fight back and use many verbal and nonverbal behaviors that appear as deception, but in fact are a result of the accuser's pestering. Bottom line: Be careful not to dig deeper on topics in which no deception was present the first time you asked the question, or you may be the cause of the apparent deceptive behavior.

One sign of deception is enough to make you concerned; more than one is usually great evidence that deception is present. In future chapters you will learn many verbal and nonverbal deception indicators. A common question is whether *one* sign of deception equals a lie. The best answer I can give is that when you see one sign of deception you should be concerned, and if you see multiple signs of deception, that is usually great evidence that deception is present. Think of it as a court trial and you are on the jury: One piece of evidence is usually not enough to convict, and often leaves room for reasonable doubt. Now pile on exhibit after exhibit of evidence and it becomes easy to convict as the doubt disappears.

Parting Words About Your Window of Focus

Moving forward through this book it's very important that you understand the concept of your Window of Focus, and, more importantly, that you use this precious time to your best advantage. Remember that the WOF is not a time to keep momentum going and move forward, but an opportunity to freeze time and see things more clearly than ever before.

As you practice your WOF, I think you'll come to realize how valuable this simple five-second interval can be, not just in detecting deception, but also in everyday conversations you have in all areas of your life.

We could all use a little more focus in our lives; the WOF provides just that.

Action Plan for Chapter 5

Now that you know about the Window of Focus, it's time to start using it actively and effectively in your daily life. I think you will find this a vital tool not just for detecting deception but also for becoming a better listener all around.

It's too hard to ask you to apply your Window of Focus during every Q & A you might have in a day, but I think it's a good strategy to use your WOF during the first question of an average interaction.

Remember that a Window of Focus has a very specific format:

First, you ask the question; your Window of Focus does not open yet. Second, you give the man time to take in and understand the question. Some men respond more slowly than others, so this process can take one to two seconds, depending on the man. Third is the response period. The moment he starts to respond, your Window of Focus should open for a short period of time:only about five seconds after question acknowledgment, you need to look and listen for signs of deception.

To put the process into action, apply it during casual conversation. Even when you're not actively detecting deception—while speaking with your grandmother, for instance—it's important to hone your Window of Focus as often as possible.

EXCITING BONUS: Go to *www.facelessliar.com* and get your free excerpt of Dan Crum's new e-book, *The Faceless Liar: Is He Lying to You on the Phone, E-Mail, Text, or Chat?*

CHAPTER 6

The Two Biggest Signs of Deception

Believe it or not, you have an unexpected ally in your search for deception: **the human body**. Try as we might to gloss over our increased heart rate, sweaty palms, open pores, or flushed faces when we feel stressed, cornered, or anxious, the body's autonomic nervous system (ANS) struggles just as valiantly to give us away.

That's because the ANS functions as a regulatory part of the nervous system, charged with regulating those vital body functions scientists consider to be involuntary: breathing, heart rate, blood flow, perspiration, and so on. As it interacts with a sophisticated series of hormones and glands, the ANS continually updates itself and responds to life's daily pressures, routines, boredom, and excitement to provide your body with the appropriate response.

At rest, during serene and peaceful times, the ANS restores the body to its natural balance, or a state of blissful *homeostasis*, in which oxygen, blood flow, perspiration, and skin color are all balanced in a harmonious state. When something such as stress, anxiety, or real danger enters the picture, the ANS triggers what is known as the *stress response*, a.k.a. the "fight, flight, or freeze" response.

When the body perceives danger, the ANS causes the glands to produce certain hormones, such as adrenaline and cortisol, to send the body into overdrive as a natural response to this danger stimulus (otherwise known as the "stress response").

Fight, Flight—or FREEZE!

As a result, your body leaves its formerly blissful state of homeostasis and enters this supercharged, almost superhuman state in which blood- and oxygen-flow are increased, reaction time is enhanced, and muscles become more limber and available if necessary. In short, within seconds your body is ready to (1) **fight** the perceived danger, (2) give **flight** and avoid it to live another day, or (3) short-circuit and **freeze** altogether.

How might this "fight, flight, or freeze" response look? If you've ever watched a lion chasing after a gazelle on a nature channel, you will see in vivid living color the same thing a man is feeling when you ask him a question he feels stress about and starts to deceive you.

Picture that grazing gazelle, content and at peace, its body experiencing a balance of chemical systems as its breathing, heart rate, and muscle response is carefully regulated. Suddenly a lion launches from the brush, and immediately the gazelle must decide to do one of three things: fight, flee, or freeze.

In milliseconds the gazelle decides this is not the predator to fight, and freezing really isn't an option, so immediately it takes flight. Its body—regulated by the autonomic nervous system—provides it with all the tools it needs to outrun the lion: its heart rate increases; its lungs produce more oxygen; digestion, bladder, and even sphincter control are often inhibited; its pores open to allow increased perspiration; it experiences tunnel vision to ignore any other outside stimuli beyond the pursuing lion; and its muscles benefit from an acceleration of what scientists refer to as "instantaneous reflex action."

The gazelle doesn't train for such immediate and instantaneous responses; it can thank its ancestors and their ancestors and on and on throughout the gazelle's—and every other living mammal's—slow and painful evolution. This response is hardwired into its DNA—ours too, as a matter of fact. That's right, we can thank our prehistoric ancestors for fine-tuning this "fight, flight, or freeze" response throughout the centuries.

Regardless of how many years have passed or centuries have dawned, the human stress response remains essentially the same as it was when men hunted woolly mammoths and saber-tooth tigers instead of beautiful ladies on the singles circuit.

Why the ANS Is Your Ally

When it comes to detecting deception, the beauty of the autonomic nervous system is that regardless of how long we've lived with it or how hard we try to mask it, we are simply not advanced enough to control the body's response to stress. These are involuntary reactions; they just happen.

Even highly trained soldiers in the field, specialists in controlling their breathing, heart rate, and muscle reflexes, cannot sufficiently cover up or mask their stress response to the point at which they can stop their faces from flushing, their pulses from racing, or a bead of sweat from dropping from their foreheads during an intense battle, or, in some cases, an even more intense interrogation.

I can tell you from experience that even with all my advanced CIA training in detecting deception and knowing the warning signs, when I choose to lie, fib, or omit something for whatever reason (not that it happens very often), I suddenly notice my body rebelling against me as my heart rate and oxygen flow increase. I have a hard time sitting still, and I tend to move to relieve the stress.

Even though I know these signs, and that they should be avoided if I am to escape detection, they are so involuntary and ingrained in my DNA that it is simply not possible to eliminate or control them. The best one can do is try to mask them, and that's where deception comes in.

When you have passed the point of suspecting a man is deceiving you and want to press him—actively and, in some cases, even agressively—for more information, one of your most valuable allies in doing so will be the ANS.

Some of you may already be doing this instinctively— it's called "turning up the heat," and we often do it when something smells fishy, or, just the opposite, when things appear to be going far too well. Even Ashley, who was pretty new to the deception-detecting game when she went on her first speed-dating expedition, instinctively knew to turn up the heat at one point in each of the four meet-and-greets we discussed.

If you'll recall, her questions were also specifically designed to induce the stress response:

- **Question #1:** *Have you ever cheated on anyone?*
- **Question #2:** *What do you think a woman should do if she finds out her man cheated?*

The great thing about such questions is that they can be generic, like Ashley's, just kind of sniffing around in general, and still create the fight, flight, or freeze response, but they can also be highly personalized if you've been in the relationship longer or are instantly seeing red flags that might indicate deception in a particular area.

For instance, for the man you think may be unemployed, you could definitely jack up the stress response by asking:

- "Do you have a job?"
- "What's your work schedule?"
- "What is your work phone number?"

Or if you suspect a man is actively in another relationship while trying to start one with you, you might ask:

- "Are you currently dating anyone?"
- "What would you think about someone who tried to date two people at once?"
- "Have you ever started a new relationship while you were still in an old one?"

When the stress response is instigated, it gives many indicators of deception, but not every man will exhibit all of them. For this reason, I have determined the two biggest signs of deception, and I will share them here as they are exhibited by nearly everyone upon acting with deceit.

Sleep Points

Let's start with the first major skill you will need to learn: **what to look for**.

Remember when I explained that your autonomic nervous system causes your body to react automatically to a stressful situation? Well, in the case of the question you asked the guy in our last chapter—"So, have you ever had a one-night stand?"—he hears the question, acknowledges it by processing it through his memory bank, and then gives you a response. Normally, he will say something (verbally), but what you are looking for is what he does with his body—specifically, certain parts of his body. In most situations a guy will ideally be sitting when you ask this question. As he is sitting, points of his body are at rest.

Let's call these **sleep points**.

Here is an example: Let's say that you see his left foot is on the ground, his right calf is resting on his left thigh, his right elbow is resting on his right thigh, his right hand is resting on his right knee, and his left hand is resting on his left ankle. Those are his sleep points—how he is sitting when he is relaxed, serene, and in control, like that poor gazelle before the lion pounces—and what we are looking for is if the question wakes up any of those sleep points.

This is the autonomic nervous system at work. You are trying to invoke the stress response and see if he will fight, flee, or freeze. If the man feels threatened by the question, meaning he believes you are asking because you wouldn't want to date him if he has had a one-night stand and he knows he has, he will have *no control* over his body's automatic reaction to wake up one or more of his sleep points.

This is very important: People can't control their bodies' reactions to wake up sleep points when they are asked a question they feel threatened by. Let me repeat that a different way: Peoples' sleep points will *automatically* wake up when you ask them a question by which they feel threatened.

So in the example of the man being asked whether he has ever had a one-night stand (or if he was employed or currently dating anyone), you will definitely see one or more of his sleep points awaken during your Window of Focus *if* this question poses a threat. Stick with me and I'll show you some of the things you might see in this scenario: The man may uncross his legs or move one of his arms or hands; any of these movements is his body's way of releasing the stress he feels as a result of the question.

Remember his WIN (What Is Normal) so that when you see the man's sleep points awaken you are not observing his normal movements or gestures, but truly a stress-induced automatic reaction to your question.

So the first major thing you want to look for after you ask a question whose answer you feel is important is whether any of the person's sleep points wake up during your WOF after question acknowledgement.

At this point, you are probably curious whether there are more things about a person's body language or nonverbal behavior you should look for or notice. The fact is, there are dozens of nonverbal, physiological clues you can notice, and I will describe in detail and give examples of each in Chapter 8.

Guilt Twists

You have a hidden ally in the autonomic nervous system, but men also have a secret weapon to help them deceive you: guilt. Not to sound sexist or politically incorrect, but men and women are different—we all know this. One significant way men and women are different is the degree to which they feel guilt.

Although many sensitive men are out there, the majority of males have a different view of guilt than do women. As Sally Law, LiveScience.com's "Science of Sex" columnist asks and answers: "How guilty would you feel if you cheated on your partner? The answer has a lot to do with the type of infidelity—and your gender. Men feel guiltier following sexual infidelity, while women feel guiltier after emotional transgression...."

Many women I've talked to feel guilty even *thinking* about infidelity, whether they've committed it or not. Women also feel guilty if they've judged someone wrongly or made a false accusation. And don't men know it! A guy who is predisposed to deceive you, or one who's been caught in a lie, knows that you feel guilty about the accusation, and guys *definitely* use this to their advantage.

Remember, it is your right to ask these questions and get honest answers. If you feel guilty every time you ask them, human nature is such that you will simply learn to avoid the guilt by not asking them; guys know this too!

Put the shoe on the other foot. If a man were to ask you, "Have you ever cheated on someone?" would you try to manipulate him into feeling bad or guilty about asking you the question? Would you become enraged, ask "How dare you?" and storm out? No, chances are, you would answer honestly, even if it was painful, and suffer the consequences, good, bad, or ugly; all you're asking men to do is the same.

Now, with this release from guilt fresh in our minds, let's move right along to major sign number two of deceptive behavior, which is in the realm of what to listen for: **guilt twists**. Using our example of the man you ask, "So...have you ever had a one-night stand?" there are two types of responses you might hear: yes or no.

This affirmative or negative response can be stated and phrased in many different forms, so I'll give two common examples of what you might hear.

- Guy #1: "No, why do you ask?"
- Guy #2: "You know I'm a good guy; do you actually think I would do that?"

Question: which guy is telling the truth? Do you think the guy who said, "No, why do you ask?" is telling the truth?

Or do you think the guy who said, "You know I'm a good guy, do you actually think I would do that?" is telling the truth?

The correct answer will be obvious after I explain major clue number two, which is to listen for what I call "guilt twists." What is a "guilt twist"? I would describe it as a verbal response that has the intention of "twisting" your question so that you feel guilty for even asking it.

Which guy used a guilt twist when answering your question of whether he has ever had a one-night stand? That's right, guy number two, who said, "You know I'm a good guy, do you actually think I would do that?"

You probably also noticed that, in addition to answering with a guilt twist, he never actually answered your question. He never said yes or no, but simply twisted it back on you, trying to make you feel guilty for asking him.

Pretty clever of that guy, huh?

You may have never noticed it before, but you (and millions of other women) fall for guilt twists all the time.

In fact, you have probably used this same tactic to lie to others, but you never had my label for it. Now you will have to listen for this guilt twist after you ask any question you feel is important. Let me give you some more examples of situations in which you might hear guilt twists, and how they will probably sound.

Maybe you have spent the last year working very hard at your job and you feel it is time for a raise. I recommend that you plan ahead, have a good case for *why* you deserve a raise, and then ask your boss directly. It may sound like this: "Boss [use his or her name],

I know that I have provided tremendous value to this company throughout the last year and I am committed to adding even more value in the years to come. I know you'll agree that I deserve a raise. Boss, will you give me a raise?"

Hopefully, you will tailor this example to your specific situation to present a strong, confident, assumptive reasoning for why you deserve a raise, and I am hopeful that you will get one if you truly deserve it. But be aware that if you have a male boss he may use a guilt twist to deny your request.

It might sound like this: "I appreciate the value you have provided this company and I know you deserve a raise, but you also know how stressed I've been with the effects of the poor economy, and with my divorce and I am too busy to think about this right now."

"No" comes in many different forms, but when it is accompanied by a guilt twist, it is easy to give up the fight and feel guilty for asking for something we really want and deserve. In this example, if you were to hear an answer similar to what this boss said, I recommend asking for clarification, as I will describe here, and get an answer, even if it is still a no. Wouldn't you rather know now that you will not be getting a raise, versus wondering whether you will when "things change"?

Let's consider your current reaction to guilt twists and how they have affected you to date versus your new awareness to them and how you will deal with them. From my experience in counseling women, I have found that the common response to a man's guilt twists is for the woman to feel guilty for asking the question, bringing up the topic, or following up on a suspicion.

This guilt is usually accompanied by an apology for even broaching the topic in the first place and for making the guy feel "uncomfortable" by doubting or questioning him.

Most guilt twists are followed by a "missing answer"—for example, "You know I'm a good guy, do you actually think I would do that?" Unfortunately, many women just stop there. But a missing answer is still deception in disguise, because you're not getting resolution on the original question. How can you combat a missing answer?

Try the following strategy:

"I respect/agree/appreciate/understand what you are saying, and I would still like you to answer the question."

Repeat the question, if necessary.

Although it's not foolproof, this response lets him know that you're not going to be made to feel guilty about what you've asked, and that if you don't eventually get an answer, the relationship isn't likely to go anywhere.

Parting Words About the Two Biggest Signs of Deception

We are entering uncharted waters here: We are moving from simply knowing that men deceive to catching them in the act; this period won't be without challenges, frustrations, and second thoughts.

The important thing to remember is that you are not the one on trial here; he is. Sleep points and guilt twists are relevant because when a man *is* trying to deceive you, trust me, these two signs of deception will give him away. But how can you tell, if you don't actively engage in pressing him a little harder, paying closer attention, and being on the lookout for these two biggest signs of deception?

Action Plan for Chapter 6

This action plan is a relatively easy one: Take two sticky notes and write "sleep points" on the first and "guilt twists" on the second. Every night before you go to bed, put one or the other on your bathroom mirror. When you get up each morning, you will know that today is a day to be on the lookout for either sleep points or guilt twists, and all that day, practice looking at people differently. Each night before you go to sleep, write the results of your observations in your journal.

You can start at work, by observing people you know and trust and how they respond to daily interactions, and then comparing those reactions with people whom you may know to be dishonest—or at least who have been known to skirt the truth. Compare and contrast sleep points to become an expert at noticing them everywhere and anywhere, all the time.

Guilt twists can be a little more challenging because they require a more active response from your test cases, but I guarantee you that the more you know about them—and actively practice them—you will start to see guilt twists everywhere!

EXCITING BONUS: Go to *www.facelessliar.com* and get your free excerpt of Dan Crum's new e-book, *The Faceless Liar: Is He Lying to You on the Phone, E-Mail, Text, or Chat?*

CHAPTER 7

Listen for Deception

Here we are, ladies: the big payoff!

So far you've discovered why some men lie, why some women fall for it, and what to do about it when it happens to you. You've learned how to Get REELL and use your WOF to take a five-second mental movie of truth versus deception; you've even gotten a great head start by learning about the two biggest signs of deception: sleep points and guilt twists.

But now it's time for the big payday, and I promise not to disappoint. In the next two chapters you are going to learn all about verbal and nonverbal deception, and, specifically, the things you'll need to listen for and be on the lookout for to really nail this deception-detecting thing. Along the way, you'll learn more than 101 examples of deception, as I promised you on this book's cover.

Remember, it's not enough just to know that men deceive; it's not even enough to know *why* or *how* men deceive. You have to put action behind the theory, and you have to put your skills to use if you finally want to catch

135

men in the act of deception and make more informed decisions.

In this first chapter of the one-two punch I'm trying to deliver before letting you loose to detect deception on your own, we are talking about verbal and nonverbal deception: the words and sounds a person makes (verbal) and the way a person uses his body (nonverbal). When it comes to both types of deception, what you're really looking for is stress.

Pam Holloway, coauthor of *Axis of Influence* and author of the "How to Read People" blog, explains: "Deception-detection is about recognizing variances from What Is Normal for the person. Lying is stressful for most people, except perhaps for master manipulators and psychotics, so the number-one thing to look for [is] signs of stress. Stress can show up in posture, movements, facial expressions, and in speech."

That's why we spent so much time determining a man's WIN, or What Is Normal. Now that you know to spend some time getting the man relaxed so you know his WIN, now that you know how to **R**eset your **E**yes and **E**ars, **L**ook, and **L**isten when you Get REELL, and now that you know to open up your Window of Focus, you are ready to discover what to specifically look for when a man may be deceiving you.

The Two Types of Deception

According to Joe Navarro and John R. Schafer, co-authors of an article titled "Detecting Deception" from an FBI Law Enforcement Bulletin, "Lying requires the deceiver to keep facts straight, make the story believable, and withstand scrutiny. When people tell the truth, they often make every effort to ensure that other people understand. In contrast, liars attempt to manage others' perceptions. Consequently, people unwittingly signal deception via nonverbal and verbal cues."

These, then, are the two types of deception: **verbal deception** and **nonverbal deception**. By verbal deception I mean what men say, a comment they might make, the answers they give, and even sounds they make in response to your questions. (In fact, non-word sounds are very important, and we'll cover them thoroughly here.) When women ask me, "Is he lying to me?" they often just want me to interpret the man's verbal answers, the things he verbalizes in his replies. But it's not so simple.

Do you want an outside perspective on your relationship? How would you like me or one of my students to comment on your situation? Visit my blog, *www.ishelyingtome.com*, and tell us your story.

For instance, when I instructed Ashley before her night out on the town at the speed-dating event, I stressed that she should listen to what the men say, absolutely, but she should also *watch how they say it*. In other words, she should look for nonverbal clues as well. We'll dig into those in more detail in Chapter 8, but for now I want to concentrate on the things men say, why they say them, and, just as important, what they mean.

For instance, did you know that by repeating your question—"What do you mean, 'Have I ever had a one night stand?'"—a man is engaging in one of the most common forms of verbal deception: *delay tactics*. What if your guy suddenly "gets religion" when you ask him a tough question? "I swear to God..." or "It's against my religion to cheat" are two indicators that a man is engaging in another form of verbal deception: *using religion*.

Always Go for the WIN

Before we dig in to the actual types of verbal deception, I just want to remind you of the process: You don't just blitz him with questions right off the bat. What do we do first? That's right, lull him into submission with a few general comments, some softball questions, and a general, easy conversation that lets him relax into his default setting.

We do this to find his WIN, or What Is Normal. After all, if you don't know what he does with his hands when he's relaxed, or how he sits or breathes or even coughs or sniffles during times of peace and relaxation, then you can't very well spot the heavy breathing or fidgety fingers when you get to the important questions and claim, "Aha! He's breathing heavy—he's lying to me!"

I'd love it if you were never lied to again; I'd love it if every time you found deception, it was a false alarm! Unfortunately, you just never know until you employ these tactics, but you must employ them logically, realistically, and in the order in which they're given.

So, as a final reminder, remember to always "start with a WIN" and spend a few minutes determining What Is Normal before identifying any of the following stress responses as pure signs of deception.

WARNING: *Yes, actually, it could be you.*

Now, I'll be the last guy to ever tell you it's your fault if a man lies to you, but sometimes you can see deceptive behavior even when a guy is telling the truth. How could such a thing happen? Easy: pester a guy long enough and he's going to show signs of verbal deception such as being dramatic or defensive, or breathing heavily.

You can't back a guy into a corner with interrogation-like tactics and expect legitimate results. That's why there is a simple five-part process involved in which you:

- Allow him to relax.
- Determine his WIN.
- Get REELL.
- Ask the questions that need asking.
- Shut up and listen!

As indelicate as it sounds, it's the last point I want to address now. You really *do* need to back off and hear his answer if you want to interpret it carefully. If you back him into a corner, ask a question over and over again, or badger, pester, and intimidate him, any guy is going to demonstrate apparent deceptive behavior even if he's as honest as the day is long.

So remember, no pestering. Ask the question, let him answer, and then observe.

14 Types of Verbal Deception

I've assembled 14 of the most common forms of verbal deception, and, for your convenience, included dozens of specific examples (or "lines") indicative of each deception type.

Type # 1: The Missing Answer

Few things are as frustrating when sniffing out a lie as our first type of verbal deception: the **missing answer.** The missing answer skirts the issue by avoiding the question altogether. It's not so much a delay tactic as a verbal shut-down; you are simply not going to get an answer.

Men who are good at this type of verbal deception throw so many responses in the air that by the time you have realized you never received an answer to your question, you've nearly forgotten what you asked! You will notice a missing answer in many examples of verbal deception. Here are some of the kinds of things you'll hear when you get a missing answer in reply to your important question:

- "That's a good question...."
- "I'm so glad you asked that...."
- "Before I answer that, do you want another drink first?"
- "You're asking *me*?"
- "Hold that thought. Now, where did our waitress run off to?"
- "Who, me?"

To avoid falling for the missing answer, one clever tactic is to pose your questions clearly and concisely, because the more clear and concise your question, the less credible a missing answer becomes.

Lastly, don't be afraid to confront him about his missing answer. If he keeps dodging the question or avoiding, just be clear and say, "I'd like an answer," or "You never answered my question." If he tries to delay or not answer some more by asking you to repeat the question, go ahead!

Type # 2: Excuses

Excuses are a deceptive man's stock in trade, his bread and butter, if you will. Eventually the deceptive male gets so used to giving excuses that they become second nature to him. Naturally, the more excuses a man makes the more he clouds the issue, dodges the bullet, and, essentially, avoids answering the question altogether.

When I think of excuses I'm reminded of the classic child abuser who, when asked if he ever beat his child responds, "You know, my wife was really the disciplinarian in the household. I mean, I was working two or three jobs to support my family; I would never have had the time to hurt anybody...."

Now, this reply is riddled with excuses. First, he never answers the question with a yes or no. Then, he tries to shift blame to his wife—*she* was the disciplinarian, not him, so if any beatings occurred, well, connect the dots. And finally, he never says, "No, I did *not* beat my children," but only makes the excuse that he was "working too hard" to ever beat them.

Excuses, excuses, excuses.

Now, this is an extreme case, but you can see what I'm getting at. For our purposes, if you ask a man why, when you call the office where he supposedly works, no one knows his name, he might say something such as, "Those nit-wits can barely remember their parents' names. And what number are you calling? I gave you my direct line and told you to call that; you should never call the main switchboard, it's run by morons...."

Again, it's the switchboard operator's fault, it's your fault for calling the wrong number, the receptionists are idiots...excuses, excuses, excuses, but never an outright denial, because then he'd actually be committing to the lie.

Excuses are the catch-all of nonverbal deception; they exist in nearly every category, but I've given them one of their own because they are quite common, and the more you know to be on the lookout for them, the easier it will be to recognize them. Here are some more examples:

- "I would never do that, I love you...."
- "I am committed to you, I don't need to look around...."
- "I'm not a thief; I don't even need the money...."
- "I'm a doctor, I take care of people, not hurt them...."
- "I love you, I would never jeopardize that...."
- "You meet all of my needs, why would I do that?"

Type # 3: Delays

Lying is hard work. Anyone who thinks juggling two or more women, having a string of one-night stands, or applying for jobs with doctored resumes is easy has obviously never done it before. Men who deceive are not in this to make their lives harder; in fact, they deceive to make their lives easier. So the fewer lies men tell, the less lies they have to keep in order. Thus, men who deceive eventually become experts at lying *without* lying.

One way to deceive without actually telling a lie is to engage in this type of verbal deception: **delays**. Delays are essentially a way for the man to buy some time, to concoct a better lie or a more fanciful story, or to cloud the issue, confuse you, or rationalize away the question altogether. After all, the fewer questions a man actually has to answer, the fewer lies he has to tell you.

Here are some simple ways men use delays when trying to deceive you:

He repeats your question. One of the simplest ways to delay answering a question is to repeat it. Sometimes they'll paraphrase the question, but other times they'll repeat it, quite literally, word for word. They may do this with a mocking tone and they may sound defensive:

- "Have I ever had a one-night stand?"
- "Have I ever cheated on someone I was committed to?"
- "Have I lost my job?"
- "Do I live with my parents?"

He pleads ignorance (or deafness). Another way a man can delay answering your question is to plead ignorance—or deafness. He may cup his ear and ask

you to repeat the question, or he may say nothing at all
and point to his ear and then to something noisy, such
as a live band across the room or a crowded table next
door. Here are some things a man might say while using this delay:

- "Could you repeat your question?"
- "What?!?"
- "It's so noisy here. Can you say that again?"
- "Huh?!?"
- "I'm not sure I understood you correctly. Can we
  go someplace quieter and talk in private?"

He stalls for time. Rather than answer your question,
the man may buy himself time by making outrageous
demands, or by complaining about unreasonable time
constraints. So he might say things such as:

- "I'm not sure we should talk about this here...."
- "Wow, can we get into that after dinner?"
- "Well it's not easy to answer that...."
- "I need some time to think about that...."

He rationalizes. Rationalization is one of the more
effective "delays." After all, he knows it's hard for you
to ask these questions, he knows you already feel guilty
about it, and he knows the answer means a lot to you, so
he knows he can throw up a few smoke screens by rationalizing his answer in a rather philosophical way. This
tactic can sound this way:

- "It depends on how you look at it...."
- "Some people might think so...."
- "In some cultures, it's considered less of a
  taboo...."

- "Where I grew up, that kind of thing was no big deal...."

He searches for specificity. If a man can convince you that what you're asking is unreasonable, unclear, or unfocused, not only can he shift the emphasis from himself back to you, but he can also hope to confuse, intimidate, or frustrate you to the point that you will stop pursuing this particular line of questioning altogether. So, often a man will ask you to get more specific, when all along he's merely trying to dodge the question. Here is what the search for specificity sounds like:

- "What's your point?"
- "What are you trying to figure out?"
- "Could you be more specific?"
- "Is that what you're asking me?!?"

Remember his WIN. For some guys, delays are part of their everyday speech pattern. We all know people like this. I have a friend who repeats every question before answering, almost like a stutter.

It's not that he's lying; he just uses that built-in speech pattern as a kind of comfort zone: "When was the last time I took a vacation? Gosh, I guess that would be...." Or, "Let's see, when was my last oil change? Wow, I suppose...." So it is important to determine if his responses are *really* delays or just a part of his regular speech patterns.

Type # 4: Guilt Twists

We talked in an earlier chapter specifically about guilt twists, but I want to revisit them here because they're such a vindictive—and effective—way of turning your guilt and/or discomfort to a deceitful man's advantage.

Remember that neither you nor he is on trial here—especially not you! These 14 blatant verbal signs of deception will give you ample tools to spot deception, but they'll be all but useless if you continue to allow men to make you feel guilty merely for asking a question and/or seeking the truth.

The statements, questions, and outright accusations that follow are all clear signs of guilt twists and should be treated as such. They should be seen as potential signs of deception and responded to appropriately. Do not be afraid to counter the deceptive male.

You *do* have business asking him personal questions if his aim is to enter into your life, you have *every right* to satisfy your curiosity if his goal is to become intimate, and he *does* need to *earn your trust* if he wants to get to know you better; these are, in fact, the basic rights you have as a human being.

So heed the following guilt twists and respond appropriately:

- "You have no business...."
- "What are you going to do next, hook me up to a polygraph?"
- "What's gotten into you?"
- "I'm so hurt...."
- "I thought you trusted me!"
- "How could you think I would do that?"
- "Whatever happened to trust?"

- "You know I would never lie to you."
- "They obviously have it out for me, and you believe them...."
- "I can't believe they make up stories like that and you believe it...."
- "Whose side are you on?"
- "I thought things were good between us!"
- "We were making good progress in our relationship...."
- "You're confused...."
- "You're mistaken...."
- "Are you trying to ruin our relationship?"
- "Why would I lie to you?"

Type # 5: Flips

We've reached one of my favorite types of verbal deception: **flips**. Flips are exactly what they sound like: the deceptive male is trying to turn, or "flip," the tables on you. In a way, flips take the guilt twist and stand it on its ear; they very blatantly try to spin things his way by vaguely making it personal.

Flips are a ploy to get the discussion focused away from him and back to you—verbal ping-pong, if you will, or even a game of tag. This way, they (a) don't have to answer the question, (b) don't look as bad for not answering, (c) take the heat off of themselves, and (d) turn the question back to you.

Flips come in various disguises, and I've included them all here for you to see what, exactly, they look like.

Accusation. This type of flip accuses *you* of accusing *them*. As you can see just from the tone of the response, it's a vaguely personal attack along the lines of "How dare you?" But be forewarned: by turning the tables and accusing you, he is actually just trying to take the focus off of himself. Here is what it sounds like when he tries to do that:

- "Are you saying that you think I did it?!"
- "Why do you think I did it?"
- "Why do you want to know that?"
- "Do you want me to confess to something I didn't do?"
- "Do you want me to lie and say I did it?"

Rationalization. By rationalizing with you, the deceptive male is simply trying to flip things around and make you look like the bad guy. In doing so, he is clearly trying to escape blame or his burden of truth:

- "I'm a logical person...."
- "Think about that logically for a minute...."
- "That doesn't even make sense...."
- "There's no way I could have done that...."

Defensiveness. The defensive male is often a deceptive male; defensiveness is a kneejerk reaction when confronted with the truth, and this type of man avoids the truth when he is on the wrong side of it. So by defending himself vigorously, not only can he try to flip things around *on* you, but he can also prove himself *to* you:

- "If I did that, prove it."
- "I already answered that!"
- "I don't have to answer that."
- "I refuse to dignify that with a response."

Cluelessness. "What? Who, me? Wherever did you get that idea?" The clueless male can't be a deceptive one, right? Wrong! Cluelessness is just one more sign of the typically deceptive flip. By asking questions and acting clueless, the deceptive male can swing the interrogator's light back into your eyes and effectively blind you to his deception. Here are just a few ways that can be done:

- "It's impossible for me to know that."
- "Are you telling me I know something about this?"
- "How could I know something about this?!"
- "Where would you come up with that?"

The Philosopher. One can almost imagine the Philosopher rubbing his hands together, staring off into space, and, with wide eyes, asking all types of grand, inquisitive questions, all the while trying to flip the attention back toward you:

- "What if I said yes?"
- "What would your reaction be, in theory, if someone did that?"
- "If I told you a story about a friend who did that very thing, what would you say to that?"

The Negotiator. Negotiation is a distinct form of a flip, a way for the deceptive male to save face while saving his skin. In fact, deceptive men *love* to negotiate; it's a power play, and they always think they're the winners. Even when someone such as yourself refuses to take the bait and essentially wins the negotiation by seeing through their flip ploy and refusing a second date, they still come out the winner because there will always be someone a little less informed to take the bait next time. Here is what negotiation might sound like:

- "I don't think it is in my best interest to talk about this...."
- "Can we talk about this later?"
- "I'd need to get to know you better to answer something like that...."
- "What if I were to say no?"

Paranoia. When a man suddenly acts paranoid because you've asked a particularly pressing question, be on high alert—particularly if he has acted relaxed and generally realistic up until this question. But this type of paranoia is just another sign he is trying the old flip—trying to take the focus off of himself and put it back on you:

- "Why would I do that?"
- "Where is this coming from?"
- "Where did you hear that?"

The Defeatist. "Woe is me," sings the Defeatist, over and over again, hoping against hope you'll feel sorry for him and quit asking him so many darn questions. Here is what answers from the Defeatist might sound like:

- "I knew this would happen...."
- "I knew you were going to think I did it."
- "Why do you want to know that?"
- "What could I lose that I haven't already lost?"

The Absolutist. There is no gray area for the Absolutist; life is either right or wrong, good or bad, sunny or raining. Here is what passes for the truth in his black-and-white world:

- "I adamantly deny it!"
- "I never lie."
- "I cannot tell a lie."
- "I am the most honest person you will ever meet."

Type # 6: Ignorance

It's always amazing to me when I hear a man act as though he's the smartest person in the world one minute, but then suddenly acts as though he can't understand English when a simple question, such as "Have you ever had a one-night stand?" is asked. Suddenly, the deceptive male goes from waxing eloquent about everything from sports to politics to movies to the economy, to not being able to understand a simple question.

When a man claims he doesn't understand the question, it typically means he just doesn't want to answer it. He does this to once again cloud the issue. It's a "delay" with a little bit of "missing answer" thrown in for good measure.

Here is what it sounds like when a man is trying to claim he doesn't understand the question:

- "Did I do what?"
- "What are you asking?"
- "I don't understand what you're asking me."

Of course, as previously stated, the best way to avoid this type of verbal deception is to take the option away from him. Speak clearly, use short sentences, and state your question concisely; this takes away the "huh?" "what?" and "I don't understand the question" options.

And if he *does* suddenly scratch his head and grow hard of hearing after you've asked the tough question, repeat it. Repeat it until he answers it. The best way to avoid the excuses is to give him fewer options to make them in the first place.

Type # 7: Amnesia

Amnesia is the great escape clause men use when being pressed on an issue. This is the opposite of being detailed; suddenly the man can't remember anything at all. The beauty of this seventh type of verbal deception is that it's selective; he can bail out on the tough questions but remember every detail of the softball questions.

This tactic is designed to make him look informative and helpful. In other words, he's not saying that he can't remember *everything*. In fact, he's sure to point out, he remembers *most* things. It's just on this particular (tough) question his memory is hazy; he has amnesia.

There are many variations on the amnesia theme; here are just a few:

- "Not that I can remember...."
- "I can't recall...."
- "Let me think...."
- "To the best of my knowledge...."
- "I'd have to consult my calendar and, unfortunately, it's not with me...."

- "That was so long ago...."
- "You can't expect me to remember everything I've ever done...."

Type # 8: Complaints

In many ways, men who try to deceive are not that different from children trying to get their way. As you and I can probably recall, when we were young and wanted to stay home from school, skip soccer practice, or avoid yet another church social, we quickly ran through our convenient list of **complaints** to get out of it.

"My tummy hurts," we might say.

"Father O'Leary scares me," we might try.

"The field is too slippery and I might get hurt," we might throw out as a last resort.

What worked for us once often worked for us again; as long as we knew not to overdo it, we had a nice bank of complaints, excuses, and rationales for getting out of a sticky situation or unwanted activity.

Deceptive men are much the same, only they run into sticky, unwanted situations every time they're pressed for more/truthful information and don't know how *not* to overdo it. So beware when a man starts complaining about room temperature, the noisy band, the bad service, and so on, conveniently just after you've asked a tough or pressing question. Specifically, here are some of the types of complaints you'll hear:

- "It's too hot/cold in here; I'm really uncomfortable..."
- "I'm sick/don't feel well...."
- "I'm just really tired—can I take a rain check?"
- "My head is pounding...."

The funny thing about complaints is that guys who use them to deceive just happen to start complaining the minute you bring out the big guns. Just do this a few times and you'll see exactly what I mean. The complainer will be fine, even-keeled, and perfectly comfortable all night long...at least, as long as you're lobbing softball questions and making pleasant chit-chat.

But the minute—I'm talking the very *second*—you get down to business and ask him something serious about loyalty, fidelity, or employment, suddenly the complaints come out like gumballs from a machine: "It's so hot in here, I can barely breathe. I'm so thirsty, can you get me some water? Can we go someplace quieter? I can barely hear myself think."

Remember his WIN. If he's a whiner he's always going to be a whiner, not just when you turn up the heat. But if he's totally free and easy until you press him, and only then does he start whining, well, that's a definite warning sign that he could be deceiving you.

Type # 9: Religion

Have you ever noticed how some guys suddenly "find religion" when you start asking them the tough questions? Using **religion** to throw someone off the scent is typical of the deceptive male, and our ninth type of verbal deception:

- "I swear to God...."
- "I'm a religious person, I wouldn't do that."
- "That's against my religion."
- "My faith wouldn't allow that."
- "In my religion...."

If you'll notice, these are also another type of missing answer; they never quite give a yes or no but only feign innocence based on religious affiliation or invoking "God as my witness." Be wary of the man who suddenly "finds God" when answering a question, particularly when he didn't seem particularly religious beforehand.

Type # 10: Details

Truthful men want to tell you the truth and answer your question, not tell you the whole story *behind* the truth. Deceptive men don't want to tell you the truth, so instead of answering your question they want to tell you the whole story—and then some. In other words, in the absence of truth they load up their response with more and more **details**, many more than are required to answer your question.

Paul Francois and Enrique Garcia, principals at Third Degree Communications, Inc., explain why some men provide too many details: "Providing more information than the question called for allows the guilty subject to talk at length about what he wants to talk about, thereby avoiding the real subject."

But this is more than just another delay; by providing too many details, the man is not merely hoping you'll forget the question with all his zigging and zagging, but he is also essentially hoping to provide such a strong alibi that the situation will be resolved completely and to his liking.

Deceptive men have learned (oftentimes the hard way) that women pay attention to details, so they give plenty of them. Obviously, this tactic works well with women who aren't looking for deception, so they've gotten away with it in the past and will be hoping to get away with it this time as well. But not anymore. Now you'll know the signs.

Here is how it might sound when a man provides too many details:

- "I was bowling with Jake, Thomas, and John, and I bowled a 126 the first game and we had three pitchers of Coors Lite because they were having a 'buy one get one free' promotion...."

- "What do you mean, 'Where was I?' I called you 16 times starting at 4:36 p.m. and ending at 6:14 p.m. Your phone must have been off...."

- "I had to work late. Three of us were there: Susie, Hal, and Sam. You can ask any of them how long I stayed...."

- "I went to dinner at Cirros last February 23 at 8 in the evening...."

Again, we all know people who just like to hear themselves speak, so for them, being overly detailed is merely a way to extend their range of speech. We all have friends whom, if you ask them, "Where'd you go for dinner last night?" don't just say, "Chili's." Instead, they say something such as, "Well, we were going to eat in but then I looked at Martha and said, 'Honey, let's go out.' We drove east on Lancaster, thinking maybe we'd go to that little sushi restaurant that just opened up next to Best Buy, but I wasn't really feeling it because I'd just had sushi with a client for lunch the other day...."

Again, all of this may be true, but do we really need to hear it? My point is, always check his WIN to see if he is one of these people. If so, you can't call "deception" on him for being overly detailed. However, if all his answers before your stressor question were short and clipped, and when he's asked about being unfaithful or unemployed, suddenly he's Mr. Details?

That's a red flag waving in your face.

Type #11: Compliments

Men don't have to wait to be asked a probing question before starting their full-on deception. The overly complimentary man, for instance, is a verbal abuser who starts in with the **compliments** early, and often never lets up.

This tactic has worked for him in the past; he knows if he gets a woman talking about her new haircut, her new purse, her new job, and the like, the chances are very, very slim that he will get tossed hardball questions.

It's not wrong for a man to compliment you. Especially on a first, group, or blind date, men are often nervous and have been taught that the best way to put their dates at ease is with a simple, harmless compliment—this is not that.

This is an onslaught of niceties, a barrage of compliments. It's not just the natural one or two compliments you'd expect upon meeting someone who is trying to break the ice or impress. This is a calculated litany of compliments design to keep you focused on everything but the truth.

As I said, some guys will just compliment you because they're hitting on you. But beware if the charm only turns on when you ask him a stressful question; this type of charm is inappropriate during his stress response. So if he's been flattering you nonstop all night, it's only natural to expect he'll do the same even after you ask him a serious question.

But, if he's been appropriately complimentary all night and then suddenly turns the charm up to 11 after you ask him, "Have you ever had a one-night stand?" well, be cautious.

Just ask yourself, is this appropriate? If you've just asked him an important question and suddenly he says, "Have I ever told you how beautiful your eyes are?" Hello, red flag! That's clearly inappropriate given the seriousness of the question and the weight his answer should have.

The overly complimentary man is often hiding something, or at least hoping not to be made to admit to something. As a result, he keeps slathering on the compliments because each one is another wall of defense between him and the truth. Here are some common statements you'll hear when being overly complimented:

- "Did you get your haircut? I love the way it brings out your eyes...."
- "Have you been on vacation? That tan really brings out the green in your eyes...."
- "Is that a new purse? It looks really expensive...."

Type # 12: Sounds

Sounds are important to the deceptive male. They are filler, padding, a little extra relief between outright lies, falsehoods, and verbal manipulation. Never forget that a man is not necessarily deceiving you to hurt you or punish you outright, but simply to get the upper hand, to avoid blame or punishment, or, more often than not, to exert power.

Deceptive males rarely know when enough is enough. If one delay is fine, two is better; if one lie is good, two is awesome. As such, sounds are the mortar they use to fill in the bricks of their lies and avoidance.

Sounds have meaning, particularly when detecting deception. Often men use sounds intentionally to their advantage. The easy laughter that follows every compliment, the masculine tone used with the waitress designed to impress you, even the whispering of a phrase to entice you—these sounds, tones, or cadences are all for effect.

Just as often, sounds can be unintentional and, thanks to our autonomic nervous system, quite uncontrollable. We talked earlier about words that didn't match a man's facial expression (frowning when saying he's happy about your new job promotion), or movements that didn't match his statements (a head shake when he's saying yes). Similarly, sounds can reveal a man's true feelings if you listen for them closely.

Before you judge a sound as deceptive, go back to his WIN. Is he a cougher, a hummer, a whistler? Has he been sniffling all night? Is the sound he's making appropriate for the situation? For instance, if you're asking him about his child-support payments or his employment status, and he's humming as though he hasn't a care in the world, that's clearly inappropriate.

Likewise, consider the timing of his noise-making. If he hasn't coughed, cleared his throat, or sniffled all night, and suddenly when you're pressing him about a potential stressor he's hacking away and blowing his nose to beat the band, well, "Danger, Will Robinson!"

Here are some of the most common sounds you'll hear from the deceptive male and what they mean:

Clearing his throat. Deceptive men use sounds to camouflage their replies. For instance, to buy himself time to answer a question untruthfully or avoid it altogether, in between responses (or in some cases, instead of responding altogether), a man might clear his throat continuously, to the point of asking the waitress for a glass of water and not responding until she's brought it. By then, of course, he's hoping you'll have forgotten the original question!

Coughing. Coughing is another useful tool for the deceptive male which, similar to throat-clearing, can be used to buy time and provide a "missing answer" to your question.

Sighing. A sigh can truly mean many things, but for the deceptive male it often means something negative. For instance, if you ask a truthful male to jump-start your car after your date he will either leap at the chance or straight-up say he's no good with cars! Either way, you know the truth. A deceptive male, on the other hand, will leap at the chance to say yes, but then sigh all over the place when it finally comes time to do the deed, until you get the clear message that he really doesn't want to help.

Sniffing. Sniffing can indicate a few verbal signs of deception. For one, it can be a habitual response to a stressful question, similar to rapid eye-blinking, a flushed or sweaty face, or a trembling foot. It can also indicate disinterest, even though the man may look interested.

Humming/whistling. A man who will frequently hum or whistle has learned that these types of sounds can put women at ease. The humming or whistling man can seem cheery or falsely hopeful, when all other indications are that he is stressed, anxious, or upset.

Voice change. When a man's voice changes mid-answer or mid-sentence, let this be a clear verbal sign that he is engaged in the stress response. During times of stress, vocal cords can tighten and affect speech or sounds, alerting you to the fact that something you have said, done, or, more than likely, asked, has created stress in the listener. Two things usually happen when the man's voice changes:

- Its pitch goes higher.
- It sounds different.

Illegible sounds/mumbling. Some men mutter while being deceptive, either to cloud their previous answer or to cloud the whole issue even further. This causes you to ask, "Excuse me?" and gives them another opportunity to respond.

Type # 13: Qualifiers

Qualified answers—**qualifiers**—are just another form of missing answers in that they don't quite answer your question. But they are *more* than missing answers because they do, in fact, answer your question—just not with any type of finality or closure.

With a qualified answer, there is always a "but," never an absolute. It's never yes or no but always some type of dance around the truth with the clever interplay of words and phrases that say, "Yes, but let me explain" or "No, but here is why...."

Here are some typical qualifiers you should be on the lookout for when suspecting this 13th type of verbal deception:

- "To be perfectly honest...."
- "To the best of my knowledge...."
- "To tell you the truth...."
- "Honestly...."
- "Truthfully...."

Type # 14: Drama

Whereas most of us avoid high **drama**, the deceiver courts it. As we all know, some people are just drama addicts; they have a flair for the dramatic, and this is why we love them. Again, this is not that. The type of drama displayed by the deceptive man is purposeful, artificial, and patently false. There is an insincerity to it that is hard to ignore, particularly when you know to be looking for it.

Absolutely, it's natural and normal for a man to comment on the weather. But to go on and on, waxing eloquently about the flowers and the birds and the renewal of spring, here is a man trying to cloud the issue—any issue—by staging a performance. And that's exactly what this is: a performance for an audience of one.

You'll notice that the types of overdramatic behavior all include the word "fake" in their titles:

Fake happy:

- "Oh, what a fabulous day; don't you just *love* spring?"
- "I just *love* it when it rains. I'm such a positive person, nothing can get me down!"

Fake friendly:

- "We should *definitely* play golf together and you're welcome to join us at the New Year's party...."
- "I've got a guy I know who can *totally* hook you up with that...."
- "Feel free to call on me *any*time...."
- "We have *so* much in common...."

Fake polite:

- "Absolutely, Sir; whatever you say...."
- "I'm just here to help in any way I can."
- "Your happiness is really important to me."
- "I live to serve."
- "Your wish is my command."

Again—and I know I keep coming back to this, but that's because it's so important to be fair—check his WIN. Some guys are just drama majors; they are very expressive and overly attentive, and that's just them.

So if he's just naturally jovial and dramatic and makes grand gestures from the moment you meet until you start getting down to business, well, that seems to be part of his WIN. What you want to know is, once you've determined What Is Normal, does he conveniently get dramatic just when you ask him something serious?

If he's been pretty low-key all night and only after you ask him something heavy-duty does he start with the fake compliments, the sudden dramatic mood swing—then look out, he could be lying to you.

Parting Words About Verbal Deception

It's a lot to take in, I know. Verbal deception is so pervasive and so commonplace that it's hard to catalog it all at once, but that didn't stop me from trying! Seriously, though, it's important that you take this chapter and its companion, Chapter 8, seriously, because these are, in effect, your playbook for detecting deception.

If you become familiar with the many forms of verbal deception and also become adept at recognizing them, you can excise the majority of male-oriented deception from your life altogether.

What's fascinating about detecting deception is that men are absolutely baffled when you call them on it. If you can get over the guilt and force yourself to stand up for yourself and confront men about their deception, it absolutely unravels them; they become unhinged. Either that or they barter, blather, or bully until the end. Regardless, verbal deception is the deceptive male's meal ticket, and when you revoke it they go hungry!

Action Plan for Chapter 7

Although it can seem challenging to categorize, let alone memorize all the different types of verbal deception presented here, it's important to start somewhere. For this chapter I would like you to use your journal or invest in a spiral-bound notebook with at least 50 lined pages inside. On the first page of this section, label it "Red Flags."

Keep the journal handy. Bring it with you to work, or anywhere you see people intimately. The goal is to use a separate page for each red flag you see that you consider to be a likely sign of one of these 14 types of verbal deception.

It's not how fast you fill up the notebook but what you do with it that counts. Every time you see one of these red flags, write what happened or, if you can, what was actually said, and then return to the pages of this chapter to find the type of verbal deception you think it is, write down why you think that, and what evidence you may have to support your theory.

For instance, let's say you invite a coworker over for dinner and her rejection makes you suspicious. Maybe she gives a really long-winded, detailed excuse; write it down. Maybe she gets mad, defensive, or personal; write it down. Then categorize it and prop up your defense through words.

The more detailed you can be in proving your case, the more you'll come to understand not only what these signs of verbal deception are, but also how commonplace they are in our daily lives.

EXCITING BONUS: Go to *www.facelessliar.com* and get your free excerpt of Dan Crum's new e-book, *The Faceless Liar: Is he Lying to You on the Phone, E-Mail, Text, or Chat?*

A great way to really become familiar with verbal deception (so you know it when you hear it) is to hear it as much as possible. Listen to the extra bonus as often as possible until you become a true Dating Detective who recognizes deceptive behavior every time.

CHAPTER 8

Liar's Moves

Nonverbal deception comes in all shapes and sizes. We've already discovered sleep points, into which I delve into more detail here, but there are dozens of other kinds of nonverbal deception as well.

You've heard the term *eye contact*, right? Well, the eyes are definitely windows into a man's soul, and when you know what to look for, they can be very expressive when it comes to nonverbal deception. Many people assume that a liar will look away when he is lying, or look up and to the right before he lies. Maybe some will, but not all.

Did you know that the converse can be true as well? For instance, whereas some men won't look you in the eye when being deceptive, some men simply won't look away! That's right, it's just one symptom of a nonverbal deception known as *abnormal eye contact*, and just one of the many forms of nonverbal deception I will share in this chapter.

Remember His WIN

I'll make the same caveat for all that is to follow in this chapter on nonverbal deception as I did for verbal deception: You have to know his WIN (What Is Normal) to find out if he's deceiving you when his non-verbal communication shows signs of deception.

We'll talk extensively about sleep points in this chapter, but for now just remember that you have to know what his sleep points look like to tell if they "wake up" under stress or intense questioning. For instance, if you've put the guy at rest and have been just talking casually about the weather, sports, movies, common friends, the restaurant's décor, or whatever, how is he sitting? Where are his hands? Is he jittery even when relaxed? If so, it's going to be hard to pinpoint exactly when those sleep points wake up under duress.

Some guys sit stiffly no matter the situation. Maybe they come from a military background, had a mother who was constantly reminding them to sit up straight, or think they're being gentlemanly by sitting at attention. Or maybe they just got out of a 23-week body cast! Who knows? The point is, you've got to figure out how he sits at rest before you determine what his nonverbal deception looks like.

Separating the Verbal From the Nonverbal

I know this can all seem a little difficult right now, maybe even intimidating. But with time, you will get more practice, and with more practice you will become more adept at detecting both verbal and nonverbal deception.

For now, it's vital that you separate the two. What is verbal is verbal and what is nonverbal is nonverbal; it's too early in the game to try combining the two and making joint assumptions on issues that should be kept strictly separate.

For instance, it's too hard to keep track of what someone is saying and doing at the same time. So reserve a portion of your discussion for verbal signs of deception and another for nonverbal. This way, you can avoid rushing to judgment and give yourself two ways to analyze his behavior.

This may be a good time to map that out for yourself. For instance, maybe on your first date you look for his verbal behavior, and on the second date you analyze his nonverbal behavior. Or maybe you're going to one place for cocktails and another for dinner; or one place for dinner and a second for dancing. Why not devote the first setting for verbal deception and the second for nonverbal?

The point is, don't try to do too much at once. It's hard enough to detect deception when you've got all the time in the world to analyze one or the other sign of deception; it becomes doubly complicated when you're trying to do both at the same time.

The more you practice, the better you will become at recognizing both areas of deception. Once you feel as though you are skilled at identifying both, you will truly be a Dating Detective, ready to Get REELL and Look and Listen at the same time.

Waking Up His Sleep Points

As we delve into our discussion on nonverbal deception, let's take a quick refresher course on sleep points. Here is an example: let's say you see that his left foot is on the ground, his right calf is resting on his left thigh, his right elbow is resting on his right thigh, his right hand is resting on his right knee, and his left hand is resting on his left ankle—so those are his **sleep points**—how he is sitting now before you ask your question. Take a mental snapshot of how he is sitting. What we are looking for is if your question wakes up any of his sleep points.

This is the autonomic nervous system at work; you are trying to invoke the stress response and see if he will fight, flee, or freeze. If the man feels threatened by the question, meaning he believes you are asking because you wouldn't want to date him if he has done what you are asking and he knows he has, he will have *no control* over when his body's automatic reaction wakes up one or more of his sleep points.

This is very important: People can't control their bodies' reactions to wake up sleep points when they are asked a question they feel threatened by. Let me repeat that a different way: Peoples' sleep points will automatically wake up when you ask them a question they feel threatened by.

So if a guy's sleep point is having his right ankle resting casually on his left knee for three softball questions, and then, when you ask him about a one-night stand, his job, or something else that's fairly stressful, he suddenly shifts that position or starts wiggling that foot when he wasn't before, or shifts from that position altogether, you have hit a cord, touched a nerve. How do you know? Simple—his sleep points are waking up!

Further Examples of Sleep Points

In the earlier chapters we touched lightly on sleep points, but now I want to get very specific about what you should be looking for—in terms of nonverbal deception—when it comes to sleep points.

Determine his WIN. Get acquainted with how he looks when he's comfortable. Remember, a man's WIN will change in time and in different environments, so it is necessary to re-determine his WIN in each conversation. Because we are creatures of habit, you will likely notice the same WIN you saw the last time you looked and listened, but pay special attention to any new things you notice.

Sitting versus standing. In most social situations you will have one of two choices:

If sitting: How do his butt, back, legs, feet, arms, hands, and head act in relation to his chair? Does he lean his body to the left or right? Which leg typically stays on the floor, and which bends when he crosses them? Where does he put his hands? Does he sit up or back? Knowing how he sits when at rest will help you pick up on how he moves when his sleep points wake up.

If standing: What does he do with his feet? Does he cross one over the other? Stand with both feet flat? Does he rest on something or lean against a wall? If he leans one way when at rest and fidgets or gets antsy just after you've asked a stressor question, well, his sleep points could be waking up.

Take a snapshot. As if you had a camera in your head, take a last-second mental snapshot of the man in question prior to asking your relevant question. Because men can and will change their sleep points throughout a conversation, it is important to notice his sleep points right before you ask that important question.

Leg movements. When it comes to sleep points, a man's legs have a lot to say. He can stand straight, slouch, fidget, or stand at attention, and if you know what his WIN is, you're better armed to spot the following awakening sleep points:

Crossing/uncrossing legs: Is he a habitual leg-crosser even when relaxed? You have to check; some guys are just naturally fidgety. But if he likes to sprawl out when relaxed and suddenly springs to life, crossing and uncrossing his legs when you ask him something serious, chances are he could be lying.

Bouncing or swinging legs: Remember, fidgeting is not necessarily a sign of deception unless he only does it under stress. So if his legs bounce or swing repeatedly when you're just chatting or having small talk, and they also do that when under stress, they're not necessarily nonverbal signs of deception.

The legs stop moving: If you have determined that a guy's WIN is to habitually cross, bounce, or swing his legs, and this suddenly stops after your important question, that is a sign of deception.

The arms. Similar to his legs, a man's arms can tell you a lot about how he sits/stands at rest and under stress:

Crossing/uncrossing arms: What does he do with his arms? Does he cross them? Let them dangle? Put his hands in his pockets? Flex his muscles? It's important to find out how he carries his arms before you put him under stress so that you can watch for his sleep points to wake up.

Bouncing or swinging arms: Again, bouncing or swinging arms are no more a sign of nonverbal deception than bouncing or swinging legs, *unless* he only bounces or swings his arms when under stress.

His head shifts. Men are typically fairly careful about how they move their heads under stress, because usually eye contact is pretty important to them. Because the eyes are connected to the head, men are usually fairly careful to avoid any sudden or rapid changes in head movement. However, the ANS often gives them away. Remember, we can't control how our sleep points wake up. So this is where it comes in handy if you've watched how his head moves when he responds to benign questions. Does he always cock his head to the right or left when answering a question? Or just when answering stressful questions he'd rather avoid?

His back changes contact with chair. Let's say you've just asked him, "Who keeps texting you?" Does he suddenly sit up, arch his back, or lean to one side? Was he sitting with his back squarely pressed against the chair before you asked him this stressor question? Most of us will sit with our backs flush to the chair when relaxed, but arch or move them suddenly when under stress.

His butt shifts in the chair. Butts, like backs, are typically flush against the chair and remain there while not under duress. When stressed, however, a deceptive male may shift his butt in his chair, from left to right or even when he leans forward. It's easy to miss, mostly because it's fairly hidden and not something you're really trained to look for. If you watch for it carefully, however, you'll see it easily.

His chair moves or rolls. Does the chair suddenly move or roll? This may be due to a sudden movement of his legs under the table (where you may or may not be able to see), or a sudden shift of his butt or feet in response to a stressor question.

His feet move. Because the feet are attached to the legs, they often mimic how a man moves his legs. It's rare for a man to have limp legs and spastic feet, or vice versa. So watch the feet carefully, particularly if you can't see his legs because they're under the table or covered by a napkin.

Changing position: Do his feet suddenly change position under stress?

Start swinging: Do they start swinging—or stop swinging?

Start tapping: Do they start or stop tapping? Sudden changes in a man's feet when under stress may indicate deceptiveness.

Gestures. We've been taught by Hollywood, pulp novels, and TV that the man wringing his hands is guilty, but that's not necessarily so. No gesture in and of itself implies truthfulness or deceptiveness. The thing about gestures is that you're not looking for gestures by themselves, but *changing* gestures. For instance, expressive hands don't mean much if his hands are consistently and unchangingly expressive throughout your meeting. Only if they sit idle when he's relaxed and spring to life when he's stressed—or vice versa, if they are going crazy all night until you ask him about a one-night stand and then suddenly they fall flat onto his lap—do they mean anything.

Hands becoming expressive: When a man's sleep points awaken, he may suddenly start—or stop—using his hands.

Rubbing or wringing hands: He may begin rubbing his hands or wringing them as his ANS springs to life with the fight, flight, or freeze response.

Grooming: Does he suddenly start grooming himself? Patting his hair down, flicking his cuffs, picking off lint? If this is a new development, and not part of his WIN, it could be a significant sign of nonverbal deception. Other hand gestures that can indicate deception if they suddenly spring to life after a stressor question include:

- Scratching at his face, hair, legs, other hand, and so on.
- Stroking a hand over and over, or perhaps his tie, his knee, a jacket lapel, or the napkin or tablecloth.
- Picking at his skin, a stain on his tie, or even his face or nose!
- Pinching, such as at the folds of flesh on the back of his hand or at his clothes.

Adjustments. When under stress, men will often start adjusting themselves to distract from the question and buy themselves time to find a suitable response or answer. Similar to all sleep points, it's not so important *what* the man is adjusting but *when* he starts adjusting.

Adjusting clothes: He might suddenly start pulling at his clothes under stress, or fixing his tie or collar. If his clothes suddenly become a preoccupation coincidentally when you start asking him a serious question, it should be cause for concern.

Watch or jewelry adjustment: Maybe he ignores his clothes but starts twisting his ring, adjusting his watch, or comparing the time on his watch to the time on the clock behind the bar. Again, ask yourself why he is doing this right now. Is it appropriate for the situation? Probably not.

Adjusting or cleaning glasses: If he suddenly starts adjusting and readjusting his glasses, or even cleaning them, to buy time during a stressful question or two, chances are something is afoot, particularly if it's all of a sudden and not something he's done several times while he was relaxed.

Fixing or straightening hair: A sudden preoccupation with his hair when under stress is generally a pretty good sign of nonverbal deception.

Nail inspection. Deceptive men will often suddenly start inspecting their nails when under stress. Why? Typically to buy themselves time. It's a natural inclination because they get to avoid eye contact for a specific reason, and it's not all that suspicious. That is, unless you know what to look for.

Biting. Some people bite their nails or lips or even objects all the time; most only do so under stress. If you've determined that your guy is a biter even when relaxed, if that's his WIN, then watching him bite a cocktail straw or ballpoint pen when under stress might not do you much good. However, if he's suddenly biting his nails, lips, or a pen during a stressor question, look out.

Cleaning surroundings. While under stress, a man may suddenly start cleaning up the table or the chairs, straightening silverware, or folding and re-folding his napkin. Again, if it's something he's been doing all night, chances are you've got a fidgeter, not a liar. But if it's something he does all of a sudden because you're finally pressing him on an issue, be aware that this could be considered a sign of nonverbal deception.

Wiping sweat. Sweat is an absolute product of the ANS's fight, flight, or freeze response. When under stress, we can't control our body's primordial responses to danger, and when preparing to flee, the body opens the pores to allow for additional sweating to cool it down during exertion. Again, some guys are sweaters for no good reason; maybe he's all dressed up for the night and not used to it, and the extra layers of undershirt, shirt, tie, and jacket are behind his copious sweating. If so, give the guy a break! However, if he's been calm, cool, and collected all night, and only suddenly starts springing a leak when you press him on his employment or marital status, beware.

Touching/covering face. When human beings become stressed, they lose their ability to control most of their fine motor skills. Although we may no longer run out of the room and down the street during fight-or-flight scenarios, we are still incapable of controlling a multitude of tiny movements that simply happen, whether we want them to or not. So look carefully for when a man starts to suddenly touch or cover his mouth, eyes, ears, or nose during stress.

Why a man covers is quite interesting, and makes sense when you think about it: Have you ever heard very bad news and instinctively covered your ears and said, "Stop! I don't want to hear that"? Or how about seeing something horrifying, such as a tragic car accident or war footage, and you quickly cover your eyes to avoid seeing more of it?

Now think about a baby who thinks it can "hide" from you by simply covering its face before saying "peek-a-boo." The grown-up male is not all that different. He will cover his ears because he doesn't want to hear what you are saying; he will cover his eyes to avoid looking at you or what you want to show him; and he will cover his face as if this makes him disappear. All of these are signs of deception to pay attention to, and now you know why men do them.

Abnormal eye contact. What we want to determine with eye contact isn't how much or how little he's giving you, but how appropriate it is for the situation. Normal eye contact equates to seven seconds on, three seconds off, then seven seconds on, three seconds off, and so on. It's not an exact science, but that's a perfectly normal ratio as determined by researchers all over the world. So, although you don't need to time his eye contact, you can get a good feel for whether or not he's being normal by following this loose rule.

He won't look you in the eye. We've already discussed how eye contact isn't necessarily a sign of deception or truthfulness, but when a guy won't look you in the eye at all, it's a sign of something!

He won't break eye contact. Remember, normal eye contact follows a 7 seconds on, 3 seconds off rule. So if he interrupts this rule one way or the other—no contact or all-or-nothing eye contact—he could be reacting out of stress and unsure of what "natural" means anymore.

He blinks too often or keeps his eyes closed for too long. I know many men who blink often or close their eyes when they think. What you are looking for is when this starts *after* your important question.

Abnormal posture. What we're looking for with posture is, once more, how appropriate it is—or isn't, as the case may be—for the present situation. For instance, if he is relaxed in times of stress and stressed when he should be relaxed, something's going on. If you're asking him a really serious question and he's acting as though it's no big deal, why? Why is he acting so inappropriately? Likewise, if you're not even grilling him yet but he's sitting stiffly and too alertly for the given situation, why? This would be inappropriate for the situation. Why does this guy have his feet up on a chair when it's a more formal situation? Why is this guy sitting bolt upright in an informal situation? This is just not normal; this equates to inappropriateness of situation. He's obviously concerned about something; there's some reason for this to be happening.

Abnormal swallowing. Immediately following a stressor indicator, our mouths dry up. Again, no matter how hard your man tries to control such things, this is just a symptom of his ANS entering into the fight, flight, or freeze response. So be alert for sudden and abnormal swallowing when there is no other reason for it; for instance, he has a drink right there, a water glass as well, and he hasn't been parched all night.

Rapid breathing. If rapid breathing is not a part of his WIN, not a part of your snapshot of his default behavior, and he suddenly starts doing it when you ask a stressful question, that's a sign of deceptive behavior. But if you weren't aware and you just now notice it, you can't be certain it's deceptive. That is why it's so important to remember his WIN and make sure you know what it looks like before you start introducing stressors to the conversation.

Controlled breathing. Likewise, if he is suddenly and visibly exhaling more slowly than usual, or otherwise controlling his breathing by breathing more loudly or purposefully, it could be a nonverbal sign of deception. He is now trying to overcompensate for his fight, flight, or freeze response by purposefully controlling his breathing. Ask yourself, *If he's not stressed, if I'm not touching a nerve, why is he suddenly so concerned about how his breathing looks or sounds?*

Trembling or shaking of the hands or body. Nerves are one of the surest signs of a man's ANS going haywire; he simply can't control these gestures if they're not part of his WIN.

A new sleep point. Because I have spent so much time stressing the importance of knowing a man's WIN and taking a clear snapshot of his sleep points before you ask any important questions, I know you would notice if a new sleep point showed up. The focus here is when some part of the man's body that is usually moving suddenly stops and goes to sleep during your window of focus. This new sleep point is a sign of deception, so make sure to notice it when it occurs.

Summary of Nonverbal Deception

Nonverbal deception can be a real asset to the Dating Detective because most guys tend to focus on verbal deception and spend less time perfecting what they do when they're not talking. This gives you an advantage when you combine both signs of verbal deception and nonverbal deception.

The goal with nonverbal deception is to be vigilant; just as guys tend to focus more on the verbal act of deception, so do women. We get hung up on what they say as opposed to what they do with their body, when both are critical to telling whether or not you're being lied to.

Let's face it, when you read the title of this book—*Is He Lying to You?*—your first thought was probably along these lines: "Oh, good, finally I'll be able to tell when the words that come out of his mouth are lies."

But, as we've just seen, lies don't have to just come from his mouth; they can come from his feet, his sweaty brow, the biting of his lip, his shifting in his seat, and dozens of other combinations of nonverbal deception. Only you can remind yourself to be vigilant in your search for these signs.

Action Plan for Chapter 8

One great way to observe nonverbal behavior in others is to watch yourself. Get a full-length mirror and just sit in front of it for 5 minutes. Don't do anything special. Don't sit up straight if that's not your way, don't cross or uncross your legs if that's not how you normally sit. Just sit the way you might if you were having lunch with a good friend or visiting with a favorite family member.

For the first few minutes, just get comfortable. Avoid the mirror. Don't look at it or analyze yourself. Just get settled in the chair, get comfortable, put your arms where they feel best, and rest your legs in a way that might feel okay if you had to sit in an airplane seat just that way for the next six hours.

Now, after a few minutes, look at yourself. Take special note of where your hands are, where your legs are, if they're crossed or uncrossed (and if crossed, which leg is crossed and which is stationary), which way your head leans, or if your weight is shifted in the chair just so. Just stay like that and examine the various sleep points of your body: feet, legs, knees, hips, waist, shoulders, head, and arms.

When you become familiar with your own sleep points, you'll be that much more effective at noticing his when the time is right.

Advanced Action Plan

Here is an advanced action plan that will help you master the concepts of this chapter. Practice mirroring and matching the movements of people you associate with. What I mean by that is to copy (mirror) the body language of people you communicate with.

So if you are at lunch with a coworker, observe what she does and then do the same. If you are standing in a bar having a conversation, stand the same way as that person. There is no need to look for deception while practicing mirroring and matching. Use this as a chance to fine-tune your focus of how people's bodies move normally and how they establish and change their sleep points.

EXCITING BONUS: Go to *www.facelessliar.com* and get your free excerpt of Dan Crum's new e-book, *The Faceless Liar: Is He Lying to You on the Phone, E-Mail, Text, or Chat?*

CHAPTER 9

Deception Discovered: The Verdict Is In

Congratulations on making it this far! I want to take a moment and acknowledge you for committing to yourself enough to read the first eight chapters of this outstanding book.

I know that this is a chapter you have been anxiously awaiting. Now is the time to put all the skills that you have learned to use. You will gain a great amount of insight by looking back at the speed-dating scenario from Chapter 1 and analyzing it in great detail.

Back when you first read Chapter 1, you were already fairly decent at identifying deception. Now, as you review it again, I think you will be impressed at how much your skills have grown and how easy it really is to spot a man who is lying to you. (I will allow you the opportunity to determine for yourself where you notice deception before revealing my own analysis.)

Let's get started!

Questions # 1 and # 2: *A Recap*

You've seen throughout this book the various forms of verbal and nonverbal deception, from sleep points to guilt twists and everything in between. Finally, it's time to put that information to use and revisit our original speed-dating scenario in which Ashley was faced with four very different men—Dave, Chuck, Phil, and Sam—who had very different responses to her trigger questions.

You'll remember that Ashley asked two specific questions of each man:

- **Question #1**: *Have you ever cheated on anyone?*
- **Question #2**: *What do you think a woman should do if she finds out her man cheated?*

At last (drum roll, please!), it's time to reveal who was the deceiver, and which man—or, hopefully, *men*—was telling the truth. But first, I'd be remiss if I didn't remind you just one last time to Get REELL again.

Get REELL—Again

Remember, Get REELL! Well, because we have already met each of the four men Ashley met on her speed date, we now have established mental images of what they look like and possible biases about their sincerity.

Maybe you've been burned by tall, dark, handsome, suave men in the past and automatically think Dave is the bad guy. What if he's not? Maybe you assume just because Chuck is young and baby-faced and wears glasses he couldn't possibly tell a lie. What if you're wrong?

Biases work *for* some men and *against* others; men know this. Some men will get a sense of your biases and play to them, dressing casually if they think that's what you believe in, or daringly if they think that's what attracts you.

So while biases help some men—typically the deceivers in the group—they also hurt others. Because Phil looks like an accountant you might instantly perceive him to be a certain way, when, in fact, once you get to know him (that is, if you give him the chance), Phil's nothing like an accountant at all.

The one person biases *always* hurt is you. Biases cloud your judgment, for better or worse—typically for the worse. So, before we move any further in this final analysis, I *really* need you to ignore what you know and Get REELL. Now you can focus more on the content of their answers (their verbal and nonverbal behavior) and less on their looks or your preconceived notions.

A Note on Scoring the Men for Yourself

Before we start to analyze each of the four men Ashley met on her speed date from Chapter 1, I'd like you to do two things: first, go back and re-read Chapter 1; second, take out your journal, a notebook, or some sheets of blank paper from your printer.

As we go through each man's performance, I'm going to pause in my findings to allow you to make your own. As you write down what you notice, I think you'll find that you're easily spotting the same signs of deception I am. I also think you'll find the exercise helpful, as it underscores your own independence while detecting deception.

The Verdict Is In: *Who Was Deceptive, Who Was Not*

Who were the liars and who were the truth-tellers?

Was it **Phil**? "As he walked over to Ashley's table about halfway through the evening, she could see that Phil had 'accountant' written all over him; from his polished black shoes to his gray, ill-fitting suit to his foggy spectacles to his business-cut, thinning hair. He seemed nervous and shy, and out of the men she met that night, he was one of the few who didn't break the rules by shaking her hand!"

Was it **Sam**? "Ashley's last 'speed date' of the night, Sam, was a tad on the young side, in his late-20s and dressing it to the hilt in skinny jeans and a simple, clean, hooded sweatshirt. His face was unshaven and scruffy, but, she decided, purposefully so; his eyebrows were carefully sculpted and his eyes a deep, rich green. Despite the age difference, Ashley warmed to Sam immediately as he sat down across from her and made himself comfortable by leaning back in his chair and crossing his feet at the ankles."

Or how about **Dave**? "*The night is starting out all right*, thought Ashley to herself as Dave walked up and broke the first rule of the event by shaking her hand before sitting down. His grip was firm but just right; masculine but not macho, and she warmed to him immediately. Dave was tall, dark, handsome, well-dressed, and sincere as he complimented her on the blouse she was wearing and asking if she'd just had her hair done."

Or maybe **Chuck**? "Ashley's next speed dater, Chuck, was in his late 30s but boyish-looking, with a baby face, wire-rimmed glasses, and a permanent smile. Although not as physically attractive as Dave, he seemed sincere and his enthusiasm was contagious."

Let's find out, shall we?

Dave

Let's start with Dave, a real smooth operator. Stop for a minute, drop your bias, and think about Dave as just a man. Let's Look and Listen as Dave responds to the two questions we want to focus on.

Question # 1: Dave, have you ever cheated on anyone?

What did Dave do after Ashley asked him this pivotal question?

Take out your journal and write down exactly what you observed; next to your observations, write down whether or not you think Dave was being deceptive. Done? Good; now let's see what I think.

Dave smiled, uncrossed his legs, and sat forward. "What do you think?" he asked cockily before snorting and saying, "Seriously, don't you think that's a little personal? I mean, I guess it would depend on what you mean by cheating."

First, let's look at Dave's **nonverbal behavior**. Did you notice any deception? I'm sure you noticed that many of Dave's sleep points woke up during the window of observation. First, both of his legs awoke, followed by his back and head. Is that alone enough for you to doubt the sincerity of Dave's response? Absolutely; re-member, when a question feels threatening to the person being asked, he can't control his body's automatic reaction to awaken sleep points.

Now, let's look at Dave's **verbal behavior**. Did you notice any deception? I'm sure you noticed that Dave used one of the major signs of deception, a guilt twist, when he said, "Seriously, don't you think that's a little personal?" This is a guilt twist because Dave's intention for asking this is to make Ashley feel bad about even asking the question. In addition to the guilt twist, what other verbal deception did you notice in Dave's response? Well, for starters, he responded to the question with a question: "What do you think?" What else? He also acted as if he needed clarification to understand a straightforward question, "I mean, I guess it would depend on what you mean by cheating." Finally, as you review Dave's response more closely, you notice he never actually *answered* the question.

But Dave, as do all men, deserves the benefit of the doubt, so let's take a look at his response to the second question.

Question # 2: What do you think a woman should do if she finds out her man cheated?

Now, take a moment to write down what Dave did after he was asked that question.

As you'll recall, Dave re-crossed his legs and hemmed a little before responding. "It depends on exactly what happened," he finally said. He then clarified his response by adding, "I mean, I guess, it depends on whether he comes clean. Did the guy apologize? Did he make it up to you? Who am I to judge?"

By now your alarm bells should be ringing and you should be seeing red flags everywhere! See how easy it is to identify deception now that we know what to look and listen for? Just as with the first question, here Dave showed multiple signs of deception, both verbally and nonverbally.

Here is what happened next: Ashley began to say, "Well, I'm not asking you to judge anyone, Dave, I'm asking you to be honest with yourself—" when the buzzer rang. As if they'd been talking about the weather, Dave leapt up and shook her hand again.

Notice how, for Question #2, Dave expressed several of our more than 101 examples of deception. Which ones? He was **dramatic**, **expressed confusion** at an apparently direct question, used **delay tactics**, **guilt twists**, and our very first type of verbal deception: **the missing answer**.

I think we are all in agreement that Dave is not a guy Ashley would want to consider dating, due to the clear signs of deceptive behavior he displayed when answering her relevant questions.

Maybe one of the other guys can be trusted.

Chuck

Before we look at Chuck, remember to Get REELL. We need to give each guy a fair chance. I know I focus a lot on this tactic, but it is easy to forget and can have a huge effect on your analysis.

For example, if you just got out of a bad relationship, you will approach relationships differently for a while and tend to have your guard up. The same applies in our analysis of these four men. After reviewing Dave's responses and feeling the feelings we have about people who lie, we will have a tendency to carry that over into our next encounter and forget that we are talking to a new man who deserves a fair chance.

Question # 1: Have you ever cheated on anyone?

"No, absolutely not, never," Chuck answered immediately without so much as batting an eye. Looking her in the eye, he seemed very sincere as he stated, "Why do you ask?" Before she had a chance to answer he concluded with a distasteful look on his face, "I have no respect for men who cheat."

What was your initial analysis of Chuck's response to this question? (Write it down so you keep it fresh in your mind; then come back.) Did you notice any nonverbal deceptive behavior? I didn't. In fact, Chuck was clear, direct, and, by all accounts, sincere.

How about verbal deception? You may be confused about Chuck's follow-up question, "Why do you ask?" Great job noticing that! Sometimes a question as a response can be deceptive, but in this case I see it as normal curiosity for being asked an interesting, rather personal question. What would you do in the same situation? How would you respond? I think most of us might be curious as to why we were being asked that, so Chuck's response doesn't raise any real red flags for me. The key here is that Chuck answered the question first and didn't display any signs of deception.

Wait a second. What about that statement, "I have no respect for men who cheat"? Clearly, you're on the ball and ready to earn your Dating Detective badge! This statement could appear deceptive if it wasn't for its timing. Remember that Window of Focus we talked about in Chapter 5?

What we Look and Listen for during the WOF is behavior and statements that occur within **five seconds of question acknowledgment**. My analysis is that this statement started outside the window, was an afterthought to his response, and was therefore *not* a part of his initial reaction.

Question # 2: What do you think a woman should do if she finds out her man cheated?

Chuck hemmed for a fraction of a second before replying, "Dump him!"

"Ashley," said Chuck after an awkward moment of silence. "I have a confession to make...I'm sorry I snapped at you," he apologized.

"It's just, my last girlfriend? Well, to be honest, we didn't part on the best of terms. After dating for three years I found out she'd been unfaithful to me for nearly two of them, and, as understanding as I can be, sometimes to a fault, or so my friends tell me, that was just something I couldn't abide by...."

Are you confused? Remember my reminder of the Window of Focus? Apply that here and you will realize that all statements made *after* Chuck's initial reaction can be disregarded. So all we really need to focus on is what he did and said inside that window.

I officially analyze Chuck's reaction as sincere. It is short and sweet and answers the question with only a short pause to acknowledge the question.

Without focusing on anything else about Chuck, I feel confident telling Ashley that she can trust that he has never cheated and doesn't tolerate cheating. I'll let her evaluate the rest of what he has to offer and decide for herself is she wants to date him.

Phil

Now that we've evened the scorecard so far—one liar and one truth-teller—let's take a look at Phil to see where he stands. Coming off a good meeting with an apparently honest guy (Chuck), let's all remember to Get REELL before analyzing Phil's responses.

Question # 1: Have you ever cheated on anyone?

Phil seemed taken aback.

"Are you seriously asking me that? Do I look like that type of guy?" he asked, shifting slightly in his chair and sounding a bit defensive. "I mean, I don't see why that matters, I would never cheat on you!"

Quick, before I weigh in, write in your journal what you think Phil's answer means. (No peeking at my answers first!)

Now, I know what you're thinking: *This guy definitely has something to hide.* You probably noticed the shifting in his chair, as the waking of his sleep points took him from sitting still to moving around. You also heard his deception so clearly, it was as if he was screaming it!

First, he responded with a question of his own in the form of a guilt twist and followed it with additional statements that didn't answer the question. Not looking good for Phil so far. Maybe he can improve with the next question.

Question # 2: What do you think a woman should do if she finds out her man cheated?

"Let me ask you this," Phil countered, sitting up. "What would you do if you found out *your* man had cheated?"

Sorry, Phil, all we are hearing is more of the same; another "missing answer" in the form of a question. Let's recommend that Ashley forget she ever met Phil.

One more guy remains: Sam. You know the drill—Get REELL.

Sam

To recap, Ashley and her last speed date of the night, Sam, made polite small talk for a few minutes until Sam's cell phone rang, and before he could embarrassedly silence it, she noticed his ring-tone was also one of her favorite songs. That brought up a lively discussion of favorite musical groups that lasted so long she only had a few minutes left when she finally thought to ask the first question.

Question # 1: Have you ever cheated on anyone?

Sam looked amused, sitting very still as he smirked and said, "No, not really. I mean, okay, on prom night my date got drunk and kissed two—no, wait, three—other guys on the dance floor, so to retaliate, I kissed the principal on the cheek. Does that count?"

Now, after writing in your journal about what *you* think this means, I'll give you my analysis. First, Sam responded to the question consistently with his WIN. You can see from the interplay between Ashley and Sam that things are going fairly well; she talks to him casually about music and carefully observes how he responds in times of no stress.

Then, when she applies some pressure with a trigger question, he doesn't suddenly transform into the Wolfman and get huffy; instead, he replies as he has throughout their conversation: he's amused, he smirks a little, he answers her question, and at the same time kind of makes a joke out of it. So far, I'm not seeing any signs of deception.

How about you?

Ashley had barely finished laughing when she finally popped out her next question.

Question # 2: What do you think a woman should do if she finds out her man cheated?

This time, Sam was slightly more adamant. "She should break up with him; definitely dump him!" he said. "Absolutely, she should find a new guy!"

Watching Ashley nod in agreement Sam added perceptively, "Hey, is that why you're here tonight?"

Now, here's the thing about Sam: He's the first guy to really ask a relevant question. Now, this may sound like a sign of verbal deception (answering a question with a question); however, he answers the question, pretty thoroughly I would say, and *then* asks a question of his own. To me this shows not just that Sam is perceptive but that he is also actually curious about *why* Ashley is at a speed-dating event.

To me, at least, this bodes well for Sam's and Ashley's future!

What This Book Is, and What It Isn't

Do you feel Ashley's pain? Do you sympathize with how she rapidly met four different men and, just as rapidly, had to analyze who was lying to her and who was telling the truth?

Well, think about it: Isn't that what happens to you almost every day?

We all face deceptive people—the salesman conning you, the colleague who wants your job, the girlfriend who wants your man, the neighbor who says your tree is overhanging on their property. In an instant we must decide who is telling the truth and who is being deceptive. Why? Simple: so that we can respond appropriately.

Detecting deception is *not* about being the world police; it is about protecting yourself through good decision-making. When you know that someone is lying to you—a man, in particular—it gives you the information you need to make quick, smart, and effective decisions. You can say no to that second date, quit wasting time on long weekends that go nowhere, and stop investing time, energy, and emotion in men who are just stringing you along.

These decisions affect every area of your life. How often have you been lied to in the past? How many relationships have been doomed because the man you trusted was lying to you all along, either in big ways, as when he said he wasn't seeing someone else at the same time, or in smaller ways, such as the fact that he didn't work or live where he said he did or wasn't employed in the first place?

You are worth more than that. You are worth the truth, and that is the ultimate reason for learning to detect deception. The last thing in the world I want for you to take away from this book is a chip on your shoulder against men. What I *want* for you to take away from this book is a systematic protocol for spotting the men who lie and doing something about it each and every time.

The tools I've shared with you will help you make intelligent determinations on a date, on the job, at home, at work, or anywhere else you travel and socialize with family, friends, acquaintances, and strangers.

It's been a long journey and we've met many a deceptive male along the way, but we've also learned that by using your Window of Focus and Getting REELL, you can also rely on your instincts—and Dating Detective training—to determine when people are telling you the truth.

What's important to remember as we wind down our time together is that we are not out to seek out and hunt down those who lie to us; it's not about putting together a great offense and having it in for guys who deceive. No, it's about having this great defense to rely on if and when a man lies to you.

Action Plan for Chapter 9

The great thing about the Action Plan for Chapter 9 is that you've already started it. Remember that journal I had you start so you could write down your perceptions of the four men Ashley met on her speed date?

Well, hopefully you found it useful throughout this chapter, but I hope you find even more it useful on—you guessed it—your very next date. Keep this journal with you the next time you go on a date—speed, blind, first, group, double, or otherwise. If the journal you started for this chapter is too big, clunky, or obtrusive, invest in something smaller, sleeker, and easier to hide.

Now, you're not an anthropologist taking notes on a gorilla in the wild, so don't sit there on your next date recording everything he says, does, eats, drinks, winks at, blinks about, and sighs over. However, when given the chance—maybe while he's in the bathroom or on the phone—take notes about his behavior.

If he's showing signs of deception, list them. Are they guilt twists, sleep points, one of the 14 signs of verbal deception, the many forms of nonverbal deception or maybe even one of the more than 101 specific examples of deception I've included throughout this book? Be specific, be detailed, and be vigilant.

Use the journal as a stepping stone. Eventually you won't need it, and will be able to categorize his responses in your head. But for now, I think you'll find it a valuable tool for use during your first real assignment as a Dating Detective!

EXCITING BONUS: Go to *www.facelessliar.com* and get your free excerpt of Dan Crum's new e-book, *The Faceless Liar: Is He Lying to you on the Phone, E-Mail, Text, or Chat?*

CHAPTER 10

The Three Advanced Concepts for Dating Detectives

You now know which of the four guys we met back in Chapter 1 were deceptive, and, best of all, why! This knowledge alone will assist you in detecting deceptive male behavior the majority of the time.

You also know something equally important: **who was telling the truth.** Never let it be said that I stacked this book with punks, thugs, creeps, and losers. Men are just like women: some good, some bad; some lie, some tell the truth.

One of the most important reasons to learn to spot a deceptive man is so that you don't waste years of your life believing his cons. Instead, now you're free to go after a really good guy and find someone worthy of you.

Knowing what to look and listen for—and even how to look and listen better, more actively—will help you identify deceptive behavior and, just as importantly, hone your instincts for detecting what *might* be deceptive behavior.

To identify those men who are really, really good at being deceptive—and, take it from a former CIA polygraph examiner, even we get fooled sometimes—you're going to need the Three Advanced Concepts for Dating Detectives.

Advanced Concept # 1: *Setting the Stage*

If you could pick for yourself the most ideal setting for detecting deception, what would it be? Would you go out to dinner, where your man might be most relaxed? Or would you be more comfortable sitting at home in your living room? Would you do it on a blanket at the park, at the picnic table in the backyard, or maybe over a beer by the pool?

Setting the stage is our first advanced concept and it's essentially designed to make not just *you* more comfortable, but your man as well. The last thing you want to do when you're dealing with an ace deceiver is to alert him to the fact that you're onto him, that something's up, or that you're wise to his game.

Remember, you can't rush these advanced concepts. Give yourself time to have an in-depth conversation, a proper back-and-forth Q & A. Fitting this interrogation in or rushing it gives him the advantage, but making sure you have time for follow-up questions and a proper lead-in ensures you can do things correctly.

The following tips will help you set the stage so that you can get the best seat in the house to either confirm or (hopefully) deny a man's deception:

What Is Your WIN?

We spent a lot of this book discussing a man's WIN (or What Is Normal), and now it's time to turn our eyes to your own WIN. Think of how many dates you've been on with this guy, how often you've talked on the phone, and what your general attitude, demeanor, mood, and tone has been with him. Don't you think he'd get suspicious if all of a sudden you just up and changed on him?

Part of the "setting" we're talking about here is where you go and what it looks like, but never forget that *you* are part of the setting as well. What you wear, your hair, your mood, and your tone all add to his relaxation—or anxiety. So let's back up a minute as we set the stage and ask ourselves: What is your background in communicating with this person?

In other words, have you been laid-back, funny, sexy, alluring, standoffish, aloof? What stage have you already set when it comes to communicating with this person? If you think of yourself as window dressing in the stage you're setting, you'll realize you don't want to stand out and set the wrong stage.

For instance, let's say you've been out on three dates with this man and now it's time to pin him down on a few select questions that have been raising red flags for you. On each date, you've been playful and flirty, provocative and charming, sassy and fresh. You've dressed this way, acted this way, talked this way, laughed this way.

So you've got to realize that's your own WIN and stick with What Is Normal for you.

Be Normal, Stay Normal

Be yourself. Or at least the self he knows after a couple of dates. If sexy librarian is your style, stick with that; if business casual is your style, don't suddenly dress like a wild woman. Don't change your makeup, don't dress up or dress down, but go with the flow of what you've been doing with him.

Now, think of the characters from *Sex and the City*. You've got Samantha, the temptress; Carrie, the smart-ass with a wild streak; Charlotte, the good girl; and Miranda, the hard-ass. So if you've spent three dates acting like Samantha you don't want to walk in on your fourth date acting like Miranda; he'll immediately know something is up!

Don't Send Your Own Verbal or Nonverbal Clues

Whatever you do, you don't want to set him off for any reason or cause him to suddenly get suspicious. So watch your verbal and nonverbal cues. For instance, I realize that confronting a man—be it about his past, a recent infidelity, his employment status, or his living situation—may not be the most natural or comfortable thing in the world for you.

Naturally you may be nervous—more nervous than you've been in previous interactions with him. That's why it's so important to stay consistent; you don't want him to suspect anything. So be alert for your own little tics once it comes time to ask the big question(s). Avoid doing all those things you were looking for in him:

- Clearing your throat excessively.
- Fidgeting or moving your hands too much.
- Talking too loudly or quietly.
- Excessively crossing or uncrossing your legs.
- Being abrupt or defensive in conversation.

Take what you've learned about what to look for in him, and make sure those things don't show up in your own conversational habits.

Make It as Ideal as Possible

Setting the stage is all about being able to see his performance; in fact, you want the best seat in the house! I mean, what is a stage but a place where an actor performs? Usually, an actor is familiar with his stage and uses it to his ultimate advantage. In this case, I want you to take the wheel and show a little control regarding where you confront him.

Ideally, you want to **avoid barriers to his nonverbal behavior**. This only makes sense because the more you can see of him, the easier it will be for you to pinpoint when his sleep points wake up. The more you can see, the more deception you can detect.

When I'd interview someone before a polygraph test, ideally I would want to sit with our knees 3 feet apart, with no barriers between us so I could see his or her nonverbal behavior. Because you are calling the shots, try to avoid barriers if at all possible.

So think about where you've been going as you get to know each other. Do you always meet at the same bar, nightclub, or restaurant? Is it convenient for you both, distance-wise, but not the ideal scene to set the stage for a confrontation?

Think of other meeting places in the same vicinity (if convenience is what makes the area so attractive to you both) and pick a place that allows for fewer barriers between you. You may have to scout out some new locations, such as a big, open Tex-Mex restaurant with no tablecloths to cover up his legs, or a generously sized coffeehouse where you can sit on opposite loveseats with just a low coffee table between you.

Ideally, you want to have full view of his body, but it can't be artificial; it needs to be natural. So don't go to some elaborate trouble to make this happen; it can't appear staged. For instance, if you walk into a coffee shop and can't sit at the two cozy, unobstructed love seats you had mapped out, well, things happen. Do not make a scene, get the manager to toss the bums out and take their seats. This is *not* setting the stage; this is making a scene! Just as you want to act and appear natural, you want the setting to be natural as well.

Start Off With Current Events

You will want to set the stage well within his comfort zone. Determine in advance what you will talk about to get him comfortable—movies, sports, politics, current events, music? You don't want to seem too calculated about this, and if he's typically an assertive guy, it may be a non-issue because he's always started off talking about something that interests him and you've just gone with it.

So if he breezes in and says something like, "Man, my boss chewed me out today," well, chances are good that talking about work is going to get him comfortable, relaxed, and calm. If he asks, "Did you see that game tonight?" it's a good bet that talking about sports will do the same. Or if he announces, "Man, my buddy and I saw *Law Abiding Citizen* last night; what a great flick!" within two seconds of sitting down, it's a pretty good sign that chatting about movies will keep him calm.

However, if he's a shy, standoffish type or respectfully waits for you to take the lead during conversation, be prepared. Ask him:

- "So, how was that concert you were telling me about last week?"
- "Seen any good movies lately?"
- "Didn't your favorite team play last night?"
- "Man, what do you think about this healthcare debate?"
- "Did you ever listen to that album I forwarded to you last week?"

These types of easy, simple, pain-free questions allow *you* to steer the conversation to a place where it can be calming, naturally and mutually enjoyable, and, more importantly, will allow *him* to pick what is going to be most comfortable for him.

Plan Your Questions

Remember when we prepped Ashley for her speed-dating event by giving her two specific questions to ask each of the guys she met that night? This wasn't a fluke; when I teach women how to become Dating Detectives I suggest that they do the same for themselves. Here is what I tell them:

Plan ahead. By now you probably have an inkling of what irks you about this guy, be it some topic he always avoids, answers that don't quite add up, or just a vague, sneaking suspicion. In advance of your meeting, prepare your relevant questions so that they are specific and fresh to you. It's important to be calm and casual when necessary to find his WIN, but it's also important to use that WIN and find out if he's being deceptive by planning in advance the question(s) you want to ask.

Keep it short. Remember that this is not an interview. You can't ask everything and anything you've always wanted to know about this guy in one sitting. I recommend asking one or two questions, tops. Maybe you have more questions to ask, but if he's being truthful, you can certainly ask them later. For now, pick your most pressing questions.

Keep it simple. Make sure your questions are simple and direct, and don't give him an option to dodge the question, delay, or ask you to repeat the question. Don't ask, "What would you say, philosophically speaking, about a man—a man who isn't you—who would sleep with a woman and then never call her again? Theoretically speaking, of course." Do ask, "Have you ever had a one-night stand?" This prevents any delay tactics he may want to use, or, if he does use them, it lets you know why.

Keep it smooth. Don't force the issue. In other words, you want to ask your questions when it seems right—not too soon, not too late, but naturally, easily, and in the flow of the conversation.

Keep it shut. Not to be too blunt, but once you ask your question, keep your mouth shut and listen—and watch—closely for his response.

Advanced Concept # 2: *Rapport*

You know that feeling when you're really "clicking" with someone you've just met? When you just "get" each other and seem to have the same tastes in music, film, food, and fashion? When, even though you've just met, it feels as though you've known each other forever? Or what about that best friend or sister of yours whom you only see a few times a year, but every time you do, it's as though you've never been apart?

That cozy feeling of familiarity and camaraderie is known as **rapport**, and when you're trying to detect deception at the advanced level, it's a powerful ally. In deception-detecting terms, one way to develop rapport is called "mirroring and matching."

"Mirroring," explain authors Gregory Hartley and Maryann Karinch in *How to Spot a Liar* (Career Press, 2005), "is a natural way to show a connection with the person with whom you are talking.... You can consciously mirror, too, to convey those positive feelings and raise the other person's comfort level."

Research has shown that people respond to those who mirror and match their own moods, interests, passions, and pastimes. This puts people at ease, and when they're at ease, they're no less likely to be deceptive—if they have something to lie about—but they *will* be easier to detect because their defenses are down.

Here are some advanced methods of building rapport:

Be more like them. Rapport isn't so much about getting him or you to feel good. It's more about mirroring and matching. Mirroring and matching is a simple, low-key way of lowering his defenses by finding common ground with your man. For instance, if, on the day you meet to ask him your relevant questions he is in a mellow mood, don't be frantic and keyed-up; try to "mirror and match" his mood by being mellow and low-key yourself. If he's talking in an inside voice, don't shout; match his tone. You will find mirroring and matching a great way to increase rapport. For instance, if he's loud, be loud; if he's quiet, be quiet. This may seem as though it will look obvious, but the deceptive male is so caught up in his deception that he won't notice.

Pacing and leading. A variant of mirroring and matching is "pacing and leading"; this is simply a more active way of finding out if someone is feeling more comfortable with you. For instance, let's say you start to do something, maybe crossing your legs or leaning forward or talking softly. If *he* starts to mirror *you*, that means he is feeling comfortable with you and is instinctively wanting to feel even *more* comfortable by mirroring and matching what you are doing. So, for instance, if you have your legs crossed right to left and you change your legs from left to right and he mirrors you, it's not so much that he's *trying* to mirror you; rather, he's become comfortable with you, and that's a great sign that you have built rapport.

Don't do anything to damage rapport. Building rapport is important, but it's equally important not to damage it. Ways to damage rapport include:

- Sounding too judgmental or preachy.
- Being a know-it-all.
- Correcting him.
- Frequently interrupting him.
- Being overly honest about how you feel.
- Finishing his sentences.
- Using big words.
- Making light of his occupation.

Advanced Concept # 3: *Trusting Your Intuition*

Our last advanced concept may seem simple on its surface, but in my experience, it's one of the hardest things for a modern woman to do: **trust her intuition.**

That's right, detecting deception could just come down to good old-fashioned women's intuition.

Have you ever said to yourself, *I had a bad feeling about that guy; I should have gone with my gut*? Or, *I had a bad feeling about that job; I should have listened to my instincts*?

Remember, there are no foolproof methods for detecting deception. The tactics in this book are based on my experience, and although they *should* work a majority of the time, they won't always.

Trust your intuition. If it doesn't feel right, don't go there. Or as Dr. Phil is often fond of saying, "Doubt means don't." If you think your husband is cheating on you, explore those feelings. Why shouldn't you? Take action to pursue something further. Don't risk letting him get away with infidelity just because you don't want to look foolish.

I'll be a big enough of an author to say this: Even if you don't see *any* of these outward signs of deception and you still feel something isn't right, go there. Believe yourself first. Sometimes the opposite is also true: A man will display multiple signs of deception and still be telling the truth. This can happen when a man plans to lie and then changes his mind before giving his answer and then tells the truth. Because there is no great method I can provide you for spotting this, you will need to trust your intuition. The goal of this book is not to get you to question yourself about every little thing, but instead to get you to trust yourself so that you have the final say in whom you date.

You don't owe anybody anything. Even if a man isn't deceiving you, you still don't have to date him. And you especially don't have to keep seeing someone you suspect is lying to you. Proof is not all it takes to dump someone; even the hint of deception could be—should be—enough to give yourself permission to move forward.

This is your life.

Take back your control and fight deception head-on.

EXCITING BONUS: Go to *www.facelessliar.com* and get your free excerpt of Dan Crum's new e-book, *The Faceless Liar: Is He Lying to You on the Phone, E-Mail, Text, or Chat?*

Index

About the Author

Dan Crum, the "Dating Detective," has a BS degree in marketing from George Mason University as well as a Certificate of Graduate Study in Forensic Psychophysiological Detection of Deception. He has been certified by the Department of Defense Polygraph Institute/The Defense Academy for Credibility Assessment, and the Joint Military Intelligence Training Center. Dan holds a Top Secret clearance from the U.S. government.

He worked for the CIA as a Polygraph Examiner, Special Investigator, and Adjudicator. Dan also worked as an Intelligence Analyst for the National Counterterrorism Center, Terrorist Identities Group, where his work was used in support of written intelligence assessments for the Executive Office, to include the president in the War on Terror.

Dan is the founder of Dan Crum International and has been coaching and consulting individuals and businesses since 2001.

Today he works as a U.S. government contractor, developing customized solutions for the U.S. Intelligence Community to better perform their worldwide operations. Dan has spent his career focused on understanding human psychology, which has included working with well-known experts and authors Tony Robbins (*Awaken the Giant Within*) and John Assaraf (*The Secret*).

Dan is a speaker on the topic of relationships and deception, appearing in front of many national organizations, including the American Polygraph Association and various crisis negotiation groups and state polygraph associations.

To learn more about the author, visit *www.dancrum.com*.